A Balanced Life

with
Source Connection Therapy

Genie Monte-Pelizzari, LMP

Disclaimer

The author is a licensed massage therapist practicing in Idaho. In no way does she intend to provide medical advice or promise any cures for any disease or illness. Rather, she recommends that you consult medical professionals of your choice for any illness or disease for which you may need attention.

Medicine and healing are two different things. The information in this book is not medicine and does not constitute medical advice. In case of serious illness consult the medical professional or healing practitioner of your choice.

During a stressful time in my life, I began working with Genie and her *Source Connection Therapy* as a way to find balance and peace as I entered a new profession. After only two sessions, I noticed a difference in my body and mind. Instead of feeling constant anxiety, I felt peaceful. Ultimately, SCT provided insights to blending my sole practitioner work with a more standard work environment. I am profoundly grateful for this insight and direction. I look forward to watching SCT become a universal treatment modality to people around the country.

S. Wiley
Healthcare Executive

....

Source Connection Therapy is one of my favorite healing therapies. After taking the SCT workshop with Genie in 2004, I now use the treatments on myself with wonderful results. I feel calmer, grounded, and in the flow with the spirit during and after a SCT session. I've used SCT in my therapy practice for six years, in conjunction with massage and sometimes as a stand-alone treatment. My clients find it especially helpful for insomnia, anxiety, integrating new information, releasing blocked energy, and for aches and pains such as tendinitis. Thank you, Genie, for bringing this into the world and teaching it so well.

Fairin Woods, LMP, RM
Founder, Port Townsend School of Massage

....

Source Connection Therapy is an important tool I use regularly in my massage therapy and Energy Medicine practice. This treatment will correct most of the imbalances found in different energy systems.

I love SCT and appreciate what it does for me and my clients!

Cindy Wright, LMP
www.waysforchange.com
206-370-4555
Seattle, WA

....

I do long distance clearing, healing, and guidance work, including angelic healing and guidance, clearing entities and negative thought forms, flower essences, reiki, soul retrieval, and connecting people with their guardian angels. I added *Source Connection Therapy* to my practice seven years ago and find it helps my clients integrate the work done and move forward into health and happiness. I value *Source Connection Therapy* as an important part of my practice, both for myself and my clients.

Lindy Swartz, RM, SCTP

Author's Note to Reader

Dear Reader,

You and I are establishing a relationship. I bring to our relationship my honest attempt to be helpful and provide you with valuable information. I also am sharing with you some very personal aspects of my life and my career. What you can bring to our relationship is an open mind, eager to learn and to understand that not everything useful is visible and tangible on first sight.

I present *Source Connection Therapy* in this book in the context of my life because I think it's important for you to understand how the therapy developed. I believe that in seeing this healing modality in terms of a real person's life, you will recognize that it can work for you just as it did for me.

I have included in the text and in text boxes descriptions of clients' stories, case studies and other examples from my practice to help you understand the nature and magnitude of *Source Connection Therapy*. I am very conscious of and careful with confidentiality. Thus, in those examples and case studies I do not use client's names and in some cases have changed non-essential facts to avoid revealing the identity of the person. I also have consulted with those individuals highlighted in this work, and they have agreed to have their story used in this book.

My hope is that my sharing the information in this book will help many people improve their lives. For therapeutic massage practitioners and those in healing arts, I hope this book helps you expand your practices and to reach clients in a new, positive way.

You will notice that throughout this book, I refer to genders sort of randomly, sometimes the masculine, sometimes feminine, sometimes both (his or hers). Nothing about *Source Connection Therapy* is gender dependent, so please accept my intention that a specific reference to a gender in no way implies that it is limited to either male or female. Please read each reference as applying to both genders.

I am always happy to hear from you. I would like to hear your thoughts, questions, and stories. Please contact me any time through my website.

www.sourceconnectiontherapy.com

A Balanced Life

with
Source Connection Therapy

Genie Monte-Pelizzari, LMP

Dedication

To my brilliant, loving, and wonderful adult children, Leah Sage Just and Rodney Tyson Just, who with their love and patience saw me through motherhood. And, to my mom, my dad and my step dad. I Love you all.

Table of Contents

List of Illustrations

Introduction

"Joy is the infallible sign of the presence of God"
French Philosopher, Pierre Teilhard de Chardin

We all are too busy with our lives. Work, family, and play overwhelm us, taking our time and energy, leaving little down time. In today's America we learn these habits at a very young age. School children have little time to simply play and learn who they really are; rather, they have school, homework, music lessons, and soccer practice. Even when school is out, kids often are sent off to educational or activity-related camps. They are kept busy. The pace of these behaviors accelerates as we get older and become immersed in the work-a-day world.

Because of this stressful lifestyle pattern, we ignore our own ability to listen to our bodies. We ignore trouble signs and often wait until we suffer chronic illness or breakdowns to recognize that we're in trouble. Even then, most people fail to listen to their bodies and ignore the clues on what is needed. Rather than turning inward and seeking their own solutions during times of crisis, people most often seek professional help.

This book has been written because we all feel a need to be connected to a source greater than ourselves. How do we live in this world and feel like it all matters? Answer: through our connection to Source, whatever we each call it. Churches, for example, originally were places that united people in this need to find and communicate with Source. The churches, before they became political, were quiet, meditative places where a person could peacefully relate to one's Source, making connections to bring life back into balance. They were places where we could gain understanding about our place in the world.

As I have written so often, Source Connection Therapy is about balance. People frequently ask what I mean by the term balance. They ask: What does balance mean? Is it the ability to walk a tight rope, or rubbing your tummy while patting the top of your head? Is it you being able to walk a straight line without stepping off or being able to hop on one foot without falling over?

I have a sign to the right of my front door that reads, "Balance is chocolate in both hands." That pleasure of a piece of dark chocolate is part of balance, being good to yourself, I think.

Balance is all of those things, of course, but so much more. In a very real sense, you are more than one person. In fact, there are many aspects to that being which is you. To overly simplify this point, ignore the myriad complexities that make up a whole person and just think of yourself as being made up of three major *dimensions*, your three *selves*.

You are, of course, the physical you—the one who can stand on one foot or walk a straight line. Maybe you can even ride a unicycle or do hand stands. If your physical self is in good health, that's great, but it doesn't mean you are a balanced person.

You also are a mental self. Your brain, your mind, is always active, driving your physical self. It keeps your heart beating and your lungs breathing. Your mind is the center of your intellect and essential skills, like walking and talking and writing. Your language, your artistic abilities, and your reasoning play a huge role in determining who you are, yet even that doesn't make you a truly balanced person.

You are an emotional, spiritual person, as well. How you feel about yourself and others or how you see the world and how you connect to it are critical aspects of your life. Your belief in God or nature or the ever-present energy fields allows you to achieve greater things, to reach higher goals, and to be a better person than if you were not a spiritual being. The spiritual you provides you with something greater than yourself, something of a higher plane on which you will learn to rely and from whom you will seek direction.

Each of your *three selves*, your *three persons*, has a gigantic role to play in identifying who you are, yet no single one can exist alone. Each of your three selves must function in harmony with the other two. The closer they all work together, complementing one another, the more in balance you are as a whole person. Balance, to me, is the uniting and bringing into total harmony all three aspects of who you are. When your physical self, mental self, and spiritual self are all in balance, then you'll find joy and connectedness in your life. That is how I see balance. To me, that broad view of balance has become pivotal in all I do. In fact, this belief in my Source and in a fully-balanced life have become who I am and how I view myself in this world.

Source Connection Therapy is a simple, gentle balancing of our body's energetic pathways that has proven to be beneficial, often pivotal, to a person's full-body healing. It is premised on the fact that unhealthy patterns can be unlearned, and that the individual has the ability to learn new, positive ways of living and relating to one's self. Through this balancing and repairing process, unhealthy physical, energetic, and spiritual patterns are revealed and can be reversed.

You deserve to be happy. You deserve to be healthy and feel vibrant. I firmly believe it is possible for you to achieve a high level of happiness and health, if you will take the time and allow yourself to be open minded.

Let the healing begin.

Genie

Illust. 1. Elderly climber. Sketch from photo by Cliff Leight.

Chapter 1
My Gift of Source Connection Therapy

I had convinced myself that when I graduated from massage school I was going to be a sports massage therapist. I imaged myself working with professional athletes, meeting exciting people, and making lots of money. That never happened and it's probably a blessing in disguise.

Instead of sports therapy, my first job out of school was in a hospital. While I was thrilled to be hired straight out of school by the local hospital to work in their rehab department, it wasn't even close to being sports massage. I worked with a wide range of people—old, young, big, little, every shape you can imagine. I was with each patient about fifteen minutes or so, which was long enough to do the treatment protocol given to me based on the physical therapist's orders, but not nearly long enough to get to know the patients or understand their underlying problems This was hard work and demanded every bit of training and energy I could bring forth.

Because of the physical and mental demands of this hospital job and the short time I was with each patient, I was forced to learn to be effective and efficient. Beyond the protocols and efficiency, I learned much about myself. I began seeing myself as a person who could make a difference, a person with something to offer people who were hurting. And, I quickly learned a great deal about human bodies.

During those busy days in the hospital, I learned that bodies seemed to know what they needed better than the heads they carried around with them. The body, I concluded, does not lie, but the mind does.

Even though it was often tough, I enjoyed going from patient to patient. I loved learning my trade and perfecting therapeutic massage techniques. I enjoyed the variety of problems I worked with and the fact that this job was never boring.

Beyond hearing the clients' words during these sessions, I sensed that I was hearing other, often conflicting things during the massage. In fact, I was! My clients' bodies were *talking to me*. In many cases, their bodies were yelling at me, desperately trying to convey what was going on with them. Over time, as I worked with clients, their bodies provided more and more information, but these clients were unable to hear that same message. I realized that if I could help people *listen* to their own bodies' messages, they could achieve greater health and emotional wellbeing without having to seek outside help. Maybe, I thought, most of these people could avoid illness all together.

I'd been hired to teach a number of courses during these years and I conducted workshops on chair massage, craniosacral and other therapies. As it turns out, the saying "we teach best what we need to learn most" clearly applied to me. Teaching, I found, forced me to look even deeper into techniques and their influences on clients. Teaching, I found, really does force the teacher to become a better practitioner with a clearer understanding of how people are affected.

As I look back at my growth over the past years, I recognize that in my own practice I have learned something even more valuable than the massage techniques: I learned to listen, to understand the person. In my private practice now it is very different from the rush of the hospital. My practice is quiet, focused, and I've become very open to listening to my clients, taking time to get acquainted with the body's intelligence and what the person's body needs. During treatments I sense who the underlying person really is.

Unknowingly, I became more open to seeking and seeing a new way of understanding. It has been quite a journey from being the person I was before I learned massage therapy to the person I am today and the practice that has evolved.

You see, during much of my life I was out of balance myself. I had low self-esteem, I spent ten years in an unhealthy marriage. My children were getting older and would soon be moving on to college or work. I felt a push from inside myself to give something back, to help create a better place in this world. In an effort to resolve my destructive life patterns and other issues, I started looking for personal growth and change. The problem was I really didn't know where to look.

I was frustrated, sad, and feeling alone and sorry for myself. I worked retail, selling sport shoes and women's clothing. I tried to become a police officer, and I looked into becoming a dog trainer. None of these efforts helped. I was uncomfortable in every aspect of my life. Taking classes like Kung Fu and going to massage school were life changing, positive growth experiences.

Step by step, even as a running shoe salesperson, I began to understand that what I really needed was to help others. People would call to ask my advice for their problems, but I always asked myself, "How can I help others if I can't even help myself?"

Events were happening very subtly and subconsciously that were directing me toward a solution to my life's issues. I was being led in a positive direction, even though I didn't realize it at the time. I was changing. I started believing in myself more. Looking back on this time in my life, I'm convinced God was talking to me. Even though I wasn't consciously listening, His message was getting through.

As if being pushed by an invisible hand, I was moving toward a life involving health care. This direction seemed to fulfill my need to help others. Based on the economics and time demands of various vocations, I found that massage school was doable. A community college some distance away offered exactly what I wanted, but it was a long commute, which I couldn't do. Then, a friend, Shannon—as if she were my personal *doorman*—told me of a massage school opening soon within blocks of where I lived. She was correct. I jumped at this opportunity. As soon as that door opened, everything became available to me. This was a life changing moment, another step that I now believe was directed by God. Finally, I was moving in a positive way. I had started listening to a voice, one that was kind, loving, forgiving, and warm. I was becoming more and more open to these messages.

Fairin , the director of the massage school I attended, offered me an opportunity to study Reiki, which is a hands-on, spiritual-healing therapy. It was developed in 1922 by a Japanese scholar. The basis of Reiki is the energy found in all life. I became a Reiki Master, even though I was very skeptical. I'm really not a *woo-woo* person, and very pragmatic in most ways—always questioning—and I doubted seriously if this type of spiritual healing was real. I openly questioned much of what I learned, including the Reiki. Yet, two further life-changing events proved to me that many of these spiritual, alternative healing modalities have validity.

My mother became very ill with emphysema in the late 1990s. She was hospitalized for a time and experienced deep depression after my brother and I brought her home. I felt as if she had given up on life. She was scared and angry at herself and her physical condition. I felt helpless as I sat with her. I wanted to help but was unsure of what to do. Without thoroughly realizing why, I applied Reiki. I placed one hand on her chest and one hand on her back. She was small, and I held her like this for only about a minute before I could feel the healing energy pulled from my hands. They became hot. The heat was tremendous. Feeling the intense heat herself, she asked, "What are you doing?"

I didn't know how to answer. My skepticism stood in the way of me understanding. I was shocked at what I was feeling. I stuttered and said, "I'm just holding you, Mom."

Within thirty minutes my mother started feeling better; in twelve hours she was up and functioning, seeming to be about eighty-five percent better. She later told her friends and others that I saved her life.

This experience had a profound effect on me. Even though I still questioned much of what I'd learned, I had discovered without a doubt that there are forces greater than ourselves that can heal, if we are open to them.

During subsequent years further training and several experiences pushed me toward a deeper understanding of alternative treatments. But, the most profound of these was about seven years after the Reiki experience—the day my mother died. This was such a life-changing event that I have no doubt it opened my mind to receiving my gift of Source Connection Therapy from God.

All of my siblings—two brothers and two sisters—were with me at the hospital where my frail mother lay in her bed, connected to a breathing bag. She had instructed the doctors not to give her artificial life support. She asked only for morphine so she wouldn't be so afraid. I sat next to her bed, as I had done years before at her home. This time, though, my mother was in a coma, although I felt she could hear me. I felt her fear and shared her anxiety. Doctors told me the end of her life was near—very near.

After we had been with mother for several hours, my brother asked if I wanted to go get lunch with the rest of the family. I declined because I'd been watching our mother's signs, looking for indications the doctor had told me would signal the end. I felt she was getting ready to leave us. I suggested we stay a little longer.

I talked with her, trying to soothe her. She was gasping for air and her body was tense. I leaned close and told her everything would be fine, that we would all be fine. I told her to not be afraid. Even though she would have totally rejected the idea, I said, "Angels are coming for you to keep you safe."

It was then that I felt her body became very still, very quiet. In my mind, I could see her *essence* move out of her body. Maybe it was because of what I had seen in life, maybe even in movies, but what I saw was a *ghostly* image. It was almost like a vapor moving horizontally from her. Even more than a visual sense, for me, it was an awareness of her spirit leaving, moving away.

Regardless of whether this was a visual image or a subconscious imagining, the event was real to me. I knew at that moment, the life force of my mother was gone and what now lay next to me in the hospital bed was her shell, a now empty vessel that we call a human body.

This experience changed me; for the first time I had seen the most primal part of our life cycle. Not only had I seen the death of someone I loved, but I had seen the very essence of life. I knew then that the spirit does not die. Again, my mind was opened to an awareness of things greater than myself.

Only a year after my mother's death, I was given the gift of Source Connection Therapy. Here is how it happened.

First, the name Source Connection Therapy came to me through a discussion with friends. I asked them what they thought I should call my massage therapy business. At the time, I was working at a resort spa, work much different from what I did at the hospitals. I stayed connected with physical therapy work by doing some in-home therapy, and two days per week I worked at a physical therapy clinic. In discussing my work with friends that night, we decided what I was really doing was helping people connect to their personal Source. I had learned that my work was simply assisting people in their healing, and that the real healing takes place in their personal connection with Source. We called my work Source Connection Therapy, even though I had no idea of the full implications of what was going to happen next.

A mere week later, I was at my first appointment of the day with an in-home client doing craniosacral therapy because she was quite fragile.

As I was nearing the end of the treatment, a *voice* inside my head directed me to place my hands at specific places on my client's body. Without questioning, I followed these instructions, placing the holds exactly where I was told. My client responded, saying she suddenly felt very relaxed.

I, too, was calm during this experience. The voice I heard was soothing, like a soft-spoken man's voice, clear and precise. It was so real.

For years, I felt that people's bodies had communicated with me, but that was a sense of feeling tension or heat or trauma. This day, however, was different. It was clearly a voice, a command telling me what to do and instructing me to do this treatment on everyone I touched that day. So, I did. For the rest of that day, I applied these holds for five minutes on each of my clients. The first two asked what I was doing, because it was different from my typical treatments. With the clients after that, I headed off the discussion by telling them I was using these techniques to prepare their bodies to be receptive to the regular physical therapy treatments. I didn't fully understand the treatment myself, but I accepted the gift.

Chapter 2
From a Gift Comes Therapy

*I*didn't discuss the events of that first day with anyone. I felt the instructions I had received made sense. Although the manner of receiving the message seemed quite strange, the message itself was clearly logical and fit within my professional knowledge. Even though I'd been a skeptic, experiences leading to this event had shown me that even things we don't fully understand can be quite real.

For example, often while working in the physical therapy clinic with my boss, Steve, we used craniosacral and other alternative therapies to help patients release emotional trauma from their damaged or stressed tissue. Doing these therapies, we frequently witnessed unexpected and profound changes in people's bodies. We had no name for these negative energies that we were releasing, so we jokingly called them *cooties*. As we applied these therapies we could see and sense the patients' bodies reorganizing and beginning to heal far beyond what we could expect from typical Western medical treatment. Thus, I obviously was open to some unusual, unorthodox messages from unexpected sources.

It was almost like holding my breath during that first day as I did the treatments. Even then, I didn't question these events because I was so stunned by what had happened and how I had reacted with such trust. That evening, I joined my friend at a local pub. As we talked, I scribbled onto a bar napkin a diagram of the therapeutic holds that had been revealed to me that day. I didn't feel crazy or in distress, but later I did recognize the similarity between my frantic drawing on the napkin and Richard Dreyfuss' building the Devil's Tower out of mashed potatoes in the movie *Close Encounters of the Third Kind*. I admit it was quite weird.

My friend, Vince, asked what I was writing. Holding up my sketch, I suddenly burst out, "Look what God gave me today."

Vince, like most people, reacted by saying, "You can't tell people that. You can't tell anyone that God talked to you. They'll think you're crazy."

I didn't know how to react. I finished my sketch and put the napkin in my pocket. I felt deflated and didn't mention it again until later that night when I called my younger sister and told her the story. Anna, a completely non-religious person, spoke carefully, rejecting the idea of God altogether. "Genie, how do you think people like Einstein get their brilliant ideas? If they are from God, I don't think He'd mind if you took credit for it by saying you developed it yourself."

I suspected she thought that soon she'd be coming to spring me out of a mental hospital. For a time, I adopted a cautious attitude, but with people who knew me well, I could be open about where I felt this came from. I could tell them this therapy came to me from my Source—God.

Source means different things to different people. Perhaps each of us sees this aspect of our spirituality in a unique, personal way. Regardless of how one defines his or her Source, I felt strongly that the depth and power of this therapy came directly from that Source. For me, the Source is God. For others, the Source may be something different—Allah, Great Spirit, Buddhist Teachings, or a unique fundamental belief structure—but the effect is the same. Once we learn to connect with our personal Source, becoming less fragmented and more focused, we gain the ability to hear and understand what is needed for us to heal and become more balanced in our lives.

Over the next few weeks, I questioned everything. I focused and asked my Source a ton of questions. I'd been so shocked to hear my Source's message that it took some time to become comfortable with it. When I did become comfortable, though, I questioned everything. I figured if He was going to surprise me with this gift, then he better be ready to explain a few things.

I'm a little reluctant to tell you such personal details about my *conversations* with God because so many people seem close-minded about the subject. As your mind opens to accept that there is something greater than yourself from whom you can gain guidance, then it makes more sense.

A few weeks after my first encounter with God's voice telling me what to do with my clients' treatments, I asked, almost demanded, "What *exactly* am I doing with my clients." The answer: I was balancing their energetic systems, and the connection points I'd been shown are naturally occurring places in the human body. I was told that by touching these connection points, we are just reminding our bodies to be connected and to shore up the body's grid structure.

I received bits and pieces of information this way. I could only accept a little information at a time because I was so in awe of what was happening. This experience was so far beyond anything I had known previously, that it was a bit difficult to handle.

I was told that unhealthy patterns can be unlearned, that sometimes we get stuck in a pattern and don't see a way out of a bad situation or away from pain. We always have a chance to change and heal, the Source told me. This made sense. In my practice I recognized that change was possible, but often people were motivated to change too late, only after pain or disability overwhelmed them. I was being guided to teach people to see the need for change and to make healthier decisions before pain wreaked havoc in their lives or before they became immobile. I was being directed by a force greater than myself to share Source Connection Therapy.

"Why me?" I asked. The answer was a straight forward, "Because you asked."

Well, okay, I thought, if I can do this, then can't everyone? The answer to this question took some time, but clearly I'm not the only person given this gift of treatment. I was told there are many who have asked and been given the same gift, but this balancing can come in many forms.

The overriding goal of the treatment gifted to me, I was told, was to allow people to become balanced so they are self-contained, not fragmented by outside influences. Life stressors—work, play, conflict, illness, accidents, and countless other distractions that take us away from our paths to joy and fulfillment—can be overcome.

"Where did this treatment come from," I asked, pressing for more information.

"From the Ancients," I was told.

I was stunned. This was way out there, far beyond my normal belief system. By this time I was a little freaked out. I talked with a couple of my *woo-woo* friends who assured me this was not so bizarre after all because there was written text about some of the things I was hearing from my Source. The Ancients, I was told, are the Elders of the Inter-Planetary

Guild. And, Source, God, a higher power, oversees everything.

I was taken aback by all of this, yet, it seemed so real and so understandable to me, that over time I accepted it. At first it seemed confusing because I'd been raised without a belief in God. Both of my parents were raised Catholic, yet they had rejected God all together. I was taught there is no God, that we are alone and on our own to pull ourselves up by our bootstraps. My parents taught me that each person had to deal with everything alone. But contrary to what I was taught, even as a child I sensed there was something greater than me, and I sometimes felt as if something was guiding me. Much of the time I didn't see it or wasn't listening. Now, my Source had my full attention.

Early during this discovery process, I worked on a woman who had many physical ailments. She told me that while she knew this treatment wasn't making her disease go away, she felt happy inside for the first time in years. As I heard more of my clients relate these experiences, I gained trust in my therapy. As this trust increased, I applied the techniques more frequently and for longer periods during treatment, always *listening* to their bodies, always alert for clues and guidance from them. Mostly, I believed, I was in some small way connecting with my clients as they were unknowingly connecting with their individual Source.

During those first years I was cautious. I applied the techniques my Source revealed to me sparingly, just a few minutes for each client and sometimes not using it at all. But, over time, clients on whom I had applied my Source Connection Therapy told me they felt better. Some told of specific changes, including feeling relaxed and better able to cope with daily stress. Some experienced physical improvement, and nearly all said they seemed emotionally and spiritually more comfortable, more at ease with themselves. Better sleep was a common benefit.

Eventually, I became quite comfortable with giving the treatments and followed the guidance I was given. I developed a useable and effective protocol and was feeling very positive about the changes I saw in my clients. They liked the new therapy, and I found it to be a wonderful adjunct to the massage, craniosacral, and myofascial treatments I frequently used. In fact, one of the great benefits I saw with Source Connection Therapy was its flexibility. I could use it as a stand-alone therapy session or incorporate it into a wonderful compliment to other modalities. In some instances, I found the new therapy to be a perfect vehicle to prepare clients for further treatment because of the deep relaxation it provided.

I also continued teaching. The Port Townsend School of Massage asked me to conduct a workshop on chair massage. I see now it was another example of being led in a particular direction. Before my scheduled lecture on chair massage, I was doing some shopping and ran into a friend, Joanne, who was a former student of mine. I was surprised to see her since she didn't live in the area. She was there to take my class. We met totally by coincidence and chatted for some time. I told Joanne about Source Connection Therapy. After class, three of the students, including Joanne, set up a massage table, and I showed them the basic balancing procedures I had learned. I told them the detailed story of how I was given Source Connection Therapy and about all of the questioning I had done. I later explained to Joanne that I was reluctant to market the treatment because it felt like bragging about myself.

Joanne's response: "Genie, this is not about you. It's about what we all need, and it's what the planet needs."

I knew she was correct, yet I still felt uncomfortable talking about it. I could see people's bodies reacting positively and continued using Source Connection Therapy at the beginning and end of all of my treatments. I applied the balancing treatments frequently to a variety of clients.

Joanne and seven other therapists carpooled over three-hundred-miles from Seattle to attend a two-day course I hosted at my home in northern Idaho. My younger sister was visiting at the time. I wondered how she would react to my introducing these therapists to Source Connection Therapy. The class was full, and the two-day session was intense.

As I spoke about my conversations with God and how the therapy worked, I was amazed at how comfortable everyone was. It seemed to make sense to all of them, with the possible exception of my sister, that God was guiding me in this treatment method and encouraging me to make a difference. This two-day encounter opened my eyes to the fact that this protocol is very real and that I could be helpful to others beyond my own little world. My sister, to my surprise, was accepting, although during much of my talk about God's messages, her eyes were pretty wide.

I've worked with hundreds of clients over a period of seven years, slowly understanding the depth and power of this therapy. I remind myself frequently that it is not about me, but about doing what God is guiding me to do. As I said, at first I didn't trust it; I remained the skeptic.

It wasn't that I didn't believe this therapeutic technique would really help people, I was hung up on thinking that I was making it up or that I was bragging about myself.

Whether a client's problems relate to physical, emotional, or mental injury, I have seen that applying the techniques found in the following pages of this book will help nearly everyone. Specifically, the reader will learn balancing techniques, including the connection points on the body. Either physically touching or imaging the connection points crossing the mid-line of the body energizes the bones, tissues, and other systems. This alignment also brings the right and left brain hemispheres into harmony. From the focus of Western medicine, the endocrine, circulatory, respiratory, central nervous system, lymphatic, craniosacral, and other body systems are positively affected. From the viewpoint of Eastern medicine, the meridians, chakras, and Qi are all brought into alignment.

Source Connection Therapy reunites naturally-occurring energetic connections in our bodies that are often broken through life's stresses. The benefit is relaxation, focus, and a greater ability for the body to heal itself. As we become more aligned with Source, we are able to hear what our bodies need. Following the guidance of this book, you will feel a noticeable improvement in sleep patterns, increased feelings of wellbeing, and an enhanced ability to handle life's ups and downs.

$\mathcal{V}$

Chapter 3
The Energetic Body

$\mathcal{B}$efore we get involved with the application of Source Connection Therapy, there are a few basic aspects of the healing process I would like you to understand. In Source Connection Therapy you'll be taking steps to allow your own natural energies to promote wellness and healing; thus, we will review the basics of the energetic body. A great deal has been written on this topic, and many on-going research programs continue to expand our knowledge of how the human body's energies work. If you want to delve more deeply into the topics presented here, I have included a reading list at the end of this book. For our purposes, however, I will provide a short examination of energy systems so the techniques of Source Connection Therapy make sense to you.

Electro-Magnetic Fields

For thousands of years eastern medicine has recognized and utilized the human body's natural energy. Modern western medicine, however, usually ignored or has been antagonistic toward the concept that a person's natural energy can be used for maintaining wellness, predicting illness, or as a help in healing the body. Most often, western medicine has regarded our bodies as not having intelligence. During the last decade or so, that trend has turned toward a greater effort by medical doctors to integrate aspects of energetic healing, including acupuncture, acupressure, and therapeutic massage. This acceptance of the energetic body by modern medicine is partially driven by the results of scientific studies that clearly demonstrate the existence of and application of energetic processes.

Dr. Richard Gerber, M.D., is among the leading medical doctors to endorse and apply what he calls *vibrational medicine*—using the body's natural energies for healing. Dr. Gerber states that the purpose of his book, *Vibrational Medicine,* is to bring together the knowledge of the mainstream medical practitioner and the spiritual domain. He notes that attitudes are changing:

> "There is a new breed of physician/healer that is evolving today who seeks to understand the functioning of human beings from a evolutionary view of matter as energy. . . By realizing that humans are beings of energy, one can begin to comprehend new ways of viewing health and illness."
> [Gerber, 43]

In Source Connection Therapy, it's extremely important to understand and to accept that humans are complex, dynamic generators and receivers of energy. This energy is ever changing, yet has frequency. Several layers and types of energy are discussed in the literature. These different levels of energy are referred to by differing names by practitioners and writers. For our purposes here we will keep it simple and refer to those energies most involved in Source Connection Therapy as electro-magnetic energies or forces.

Barbara Brennan, in her work *Hands of Light,* examines levels of energy that exist among all matter as the Universal Energy Field (UEF). The Human Energy Field, Brennan writes, "is that part of the UEF associated with the human body." [*Hands of Light,* 41]. Source Connection Therapy depends on the existence and functioning of the Human Energy Field (HEF).

Some practicing healers and writers refer to the Human Energy Field as an aura. Many of the most sensitive healers, such as Donna Eden and Barbara Brennan, have seen the form, color, and texture of these energy fields and have described them in detail. Their descriptions and illustrations of auras are similar, and in every case they involve the fact that the energy fields, auras, are dynamic and vary in size, color, and shape in relation to the person's state of mind and attitude. Aura readers consistently say there are noticeable shifts in the aura when a person is in distress. Environmental changes also can affect the aura. Aura readers unequivocally say that energy fields have frequencies.

Barbara Brennan, in *Hands of Light,* describes seven layers of auras:
1. Physical
2. Emotional (with respect to self)
3. Rational mind

   4. Relations with others
   5. Divine will within
   6. Divine love, spiritual ecstasy
   7. Divine mind, serenity

The aura is an intangible force surrounding the body. The layers of the aura are often associated with the Chakras. Some aura readers describe the colors of the aura corresponding with the Chakras. Some suggest that the auras' colors are not directly connected with the Chakras. Either way, for Source Connection Therapy if you are sensitive to auras you may sense or see changes in the aura and its color during treatment. This auric shift is a result of balancing the electro-magnetic field and opening the Chakras.

Even for practitioners who cannot see the auras, most of us can feel the energy forces and gather information about a person's body from that. I often can sense the mood or attitude of a client simply from touching her or him. I can learn about the client's state of wellness and balance from these energies. It is, you see, through the electro-magnetic fields that our bodies, minds, and spirits can communicate.

Our goal in Source Connection Therapy is to balance all these energies with one another and with the world outside. For you to understand the aspects of our beings that we are considering during discussions of balance, I offer the following brief descriptions.

The body is an active energy generator. Many of the touch therapies work because of this energy. From diagnosis of problems to resolving them through therapy, understanding the energetic body is critical. This understanding is true of Source Connection Therapy, as well as other alternative medical treatments.

Electricity is generated mechanically for our homes or by the alternator in our cars by interaction of electro-magnetic forces. In much more complex ways, our bodies produce measurable levels of electro-magnetic energy. That this electro-magnetic field exists is not disputed by science. Since the fields cannot be seen without instrumentation, however, some skeptics minimize the importance of our electro-magnetic energies. These skeptics consider the electrical currents that can be measured as brain waves or as a function of the heart working are simply limited to each of those organs and do not interact or impact the rest of our minds and bodies.

When I hear skeptics talk about how these electro-magnetic fields cannot be true because they are invisible, I remind them it wasn't many decades ago that medical people didn't understand germs. Because bacteria were invisible to the naked eye, doctors were slow to make the connection between unsanitary conditions, infection, and death. Until the development of the microscope, which allowed people to see the germs, doctors practiced little or no sanitary procedures, even during surgery. Even after the microscope was in use, it took time for medical science to understand how the bacteria they now saw caused the infection. And, it took even longer for them to learn how to prevent infection.

Maybe those concerned with the energetic body have only recently reached the level of development of our *microscope.* For most practitioners of healing arts, understanding the body's electro-magnetic fields has become central to wellness and healing. Perhaps that is because most of us can feel and sense that energy. Through experience, we have learned the patterns and frequencies of the energetic fields. We have found through touching hundreds of clients that changes in those electro-magnetic fields directly mean changes in the client's health and mental wellness. In recent years, technology has allowed others to *see* these electro-magnetic fields and has provided the tools researchers needed to further our understanding of the energetic body.

That the body has energy fields and that these fields can be used to enhance health are well-known and quite well demonstrated in current health-related literature. Science has known for some time that electrical energy is generated by the brain. But, this is not the only source of energy in our bodies; rather, the heart, for example, is now recognized as the source of abundant energy. We also know that balance of these body energies is critical to mental, emotional, and physical health.

Research by Dr. Rollin McCraty and others supports the existence and importance of our bodies' electro-magnetic forces, and also explains the interaction of these fields between major physical systems. The authors explain that scientific evidence is clear that the electro-magnetic forces of the brain and of the heart interact, and each impacts the other. They further explain that signals sent by the heart to our brains influence perceptive, cognitive, and even emotional processing. [McCraty, 15-16].

The electro-magnetic energy from the heart impacts every cell in the body, including the brain. The heart's energy directly influences every organ and system, and its rhythm adjusts to changing conditions and needs. McCraty demonstrates that in addition to adjusting to maintain bodily functions, the heart's electro-magnetic fields send information throughout the body pertaining to the person's emotional state. [McCraty, 16]. These changes in the heart's energy can be measured and show a dramatic change as the person's mood and emotions change. Dramatic changes in the heart's energy fields occur as a client's emotions change between positive and negative states.

Donna Eden describes seeing a person's aura changing from being the size of a room when in a positive, balanced state, to drawing inward and collapsing around the body when the same person's mood changes to negative. [Eden, 187]. Likewise, using sensitive instruments to measure a person's electro-magnetic fields, researchers confirm significant frequency changes result from the person's emotional changes.

That the heart produces energy in relation to one's emotions is extremely important when considering Source Connection Therapy, because the energy fields are indicators of balance. Example: during times of stress, frustration, or anger, the heart's rhythms become erratic and variable, causing an unbalanced condition in other organs and physical systems. A positive emotion, on the other hand, will result in the heart settling into a steady rhythm, generating and transmitting to the brain and other organs an organized energy field. The result of the organized energy field is that various physical systems are brought into harmony and mental functions smooth out, allowing for enhanced mental performance, opening our minds to receive important information from Source.

A common misconception is that the brain, not the heart, is the source of all cognitive functioning and as such has the stronger electrical and magnetic energy fields. This incorrect belief ignores the interaction between the heart and the brain. Dr. Gerber's research shows undoubtedly that the brain can impact mechanisms that regulate the body. [Gerber, 32]. Further research from several sources likewise shows that the brain is impacted by energies from the body, including the heart.

Furthermore, recent research shows very clearly that not only is there a more direct link between the energies of the heart and the brain, but that the electro-magnetic energy produced by the heart is significantly stronger than that produced by the brain. McCraty shows that the electronic component of the heart's energy is about sixty times stronger than that of the brain, while the heart's magnetic component of energy is a whopping five-thousand times stronger than the magnetic field of the brain. [McCraty, 16].

Recognizing that there clearly is an interaction of the electro-magnetic forces within one's body is very important to Source Connection Therapy. During treatments you will see that aligning the forces and using them to remind the body to make energetic connections is fundamental. Moreover, we learn that if the electro-magnetic forces create interactions within the body, they also have influences beyond the body. In fact, these electro-magnetic forces will impact other people with whom we come in contact, will form the connection with our individual Source, and will form a connection between each of us and our environment.

We've heard the expression that a person is sending out *positive vibes*. We sometimes feel as if being around a certain person makes us feel good, or that a *magnetic attraction* resulted in love at first sight. We know from research that these may be accurate statements based in scientific reality. Dr. McCraty, for example, reports on experiments that demonstrate that a person's electro-magnetic energy can actually be measured using sensitive instruments up to five feet away from the person. In fact, these data show that the *heart energies* of two people can interact between them when they are five feet apart and not physically touching or verbally communicating.

Barbara Brennan describes an accepted measurement of the electro-magnetic fields around the body by use of a device called a *Squid* — super conducting quantum interference device. These electro-magnetic fields can be detected and measured by this method without ever touching the body; thus, further proving the existence and importance of the electro-magnetic fields. [*Hands of Light*, 20].

An intriguing and informative book by Dr. Jill Bolte Taylor tells the story of her having a stroke, which rendered the left side of her brain inactive. Dr. Taylor is a brain scientist, a neuroanatomist, and as such explains in incredible detail and clarity her feelings during the stroke and her long recovery. I find this book so amazing on several levels, and you'll read more about it later. Regarding the energetic body and how we can influence others by our energy, I found one paragraph in *My Stroke of Insight* quite interesting. Dr. Taylor's left brain hemisphere stroke had rendered her unable to speak, yet visitors during the early stages of her recovery had direct impacts on her because of their energy. She writes about her needs:

> "... but, I needed my visitors to bring me their positive energy. Since conversation is obviously out of the question, I appreciated when people came in for a few minutes, took my hands in theirs, and shared softly and slowly how they were doing, what they were thinking, and how they believed in my ability to recover. It was very difficult for me to cope with people who came in with high anxious energy. I really needed people to take responsibility for the kind of energy they brought me. We encouraged everyone to soften their brow, open their heart, and bring me their love. Extremely nervous, anxious or angry people were counter-productive to my healing." [Taylor, 120]

Our energy, whether well organized and positive, or erratic and negative, will affect those around us, especially those we touch during treatments or intimacy. When you are balanced and your electro-magnetic energy is smooth and organized, you will have a beneficial, positive impact on others and your environment. Among other goals, achieving that smooth, positive electro-magnetic energy field is an objective of Source Connection Therapy.

A professional musician friend of mine explained one night that a reason one person reacts positively to certain songs while other people do not is often because the rhythm or beat of that song matches the listener's naturally-occurring physical and emotional rhythm. When the energies of the music correspond and mesh with the physical and emotional energies of the listener, a positive communication is established. The two are in balance. With Source Connection Therapy, we are attempting to establish that positive balance between ourselves and the world around us. When we are balanced, we face the world and those with whom we interact with a strong positive electro-magnetic energy field. Just like with the music, we establish an energetic communication within ourselves, with others, and with our world. When we are unbalanced, producing erratic, chaotic energies, those connections with others and our environment are not possible, or at best are negative and destructive. When out of balance, the communication among various parts of our physical, mental, and emotional selves breaks down, rendering us less than healthy.

A person whose physical, mental, and emotional states are in balance not only will face the world in a positive manner, but will be open to the outside world and to Source to receive important information. Through balanced energies of the brain and the heart fields, a subtle yet important type of nonverbal communication will exist. A balanced person will be sending positive messages and will be able to receive information coming from outside. [Illustration 3-1]

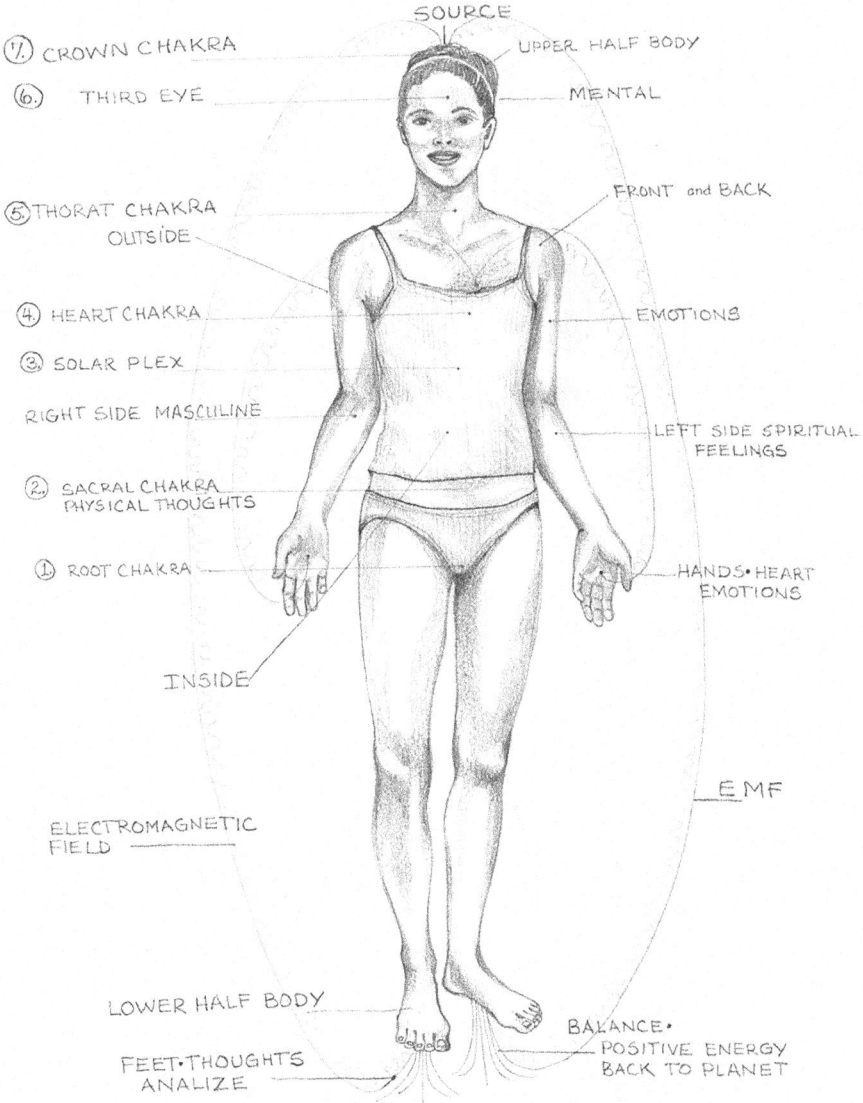

Illust. 3-1. The balanced energetic body.

Although some will think it irrelevant to our understanding of people, this nonverbal exchange of energies quite easily can be seen between humans and certain animals. No one has demonstrated this energetic communication between people and dogs better than Cesar Millan, the Dog Whisperer. Some, like McCraty and his team might argue that the energy exchange is through the heart field. Others, only that subtle physical movements or nonverbal body language trigger a dog's reaction. From either point of view, the impact is the same—human and dog begin working together, sharing positive energy.

Millan also accurately demonstrates that a person's energy, not his or her words, will impact a dog's behavior. A dog knows how we feel by our energy, not by our words. Much of Millan's work is based squarely on the proven concept of balancing our emotions and energies, presenting ourselves to our dogs as positive, calm, and assertive. Reaching this level of control, whether with an animal, a fellow human, or even within ourselves, is done through control and balancing of our energies, including our electro-magnetic fields. This balancing is the core principle of Source Connection Therapy.

As Cesar explains in relation to working out issues between people and dogs, and as I often explain to my clients who have interpersonal issues with siblings, spouses, or others, progress will be achieved and beneficial communication will occur only through calm, assertive behavior. This type of behavior can be achieved only through balancing all aspects of our personal beings—physical, mental, and spiritual. When we are balanced, we can achieve the calm, assertive demeanor needed for effective communication because our electro-magnetic energy is optimal, organized, and steady.

Energy is Communication

"The thing about energy is, talking or writing about it doesn't always cut it when it comes to truly getting how it applies to you and your everyday life. That's why dogs are such an amazing gift to us ... our dogs are our emotional mirrors. If we are unsure of how we are feeling or what energy we are projecting at any given moment, all we have to do is look to our dogs to figure it out. They will often understand us much more deeply than we understand ourselves." [Millan, 198-99].

"Animals in general respect a certain energy, and they
relax around a type of energy that I call calm-assertive
energy. They are programmed to respect and trust
this energy. This is why I believe Mother Nature is
perfect, because all animals except humans are attracted
to certain frequencies and driven to make certain
connections that are going to help them survive. We are
the only animal that can be fooled by the mask of certain
energy, or can be attracted to an energy that is not calm
and assertive, or in fact, is actually negative or bad for
our survival."
[Millan, 203].

"You will never have to tell your dog that you are sad,
happy, angry or relaxed. He already knows—usually long
before you do." [Millan, 203].

We've heard people refer to relationships as *magnetic* or experiences as *electric*. These statements may be more real than many imagine. As we encounter others or when we touch another person, there is a flow of electro-magnetic energy between us. When both are in a balanced state, with heart field and brain field energies producing positive, steady energy waves, the experience will be very positive to both people. If, however, one or both people is in an unbalanced state and the energy fields are erratic and negative, the experience most likely will be unpleasant at best. Through daily balancing with Source Connection Therapy, you can face the world and interact with others in a positive, balanced state. You have a choice.

The work that I and others are doing may appear to come from an intangible source, but the results are very tangible. Sometimes, for example, a treatment may seem like a quiet time, with little obvious physical indicators or changes. Yet these sessions are having a profound impact on the body's ability to heal itself and to deal with outside obstacles.

Physical Systems

Humans have a variety of very complex systems. If any one of these systems is out of balance, all energetic and physical systems are affected to varying degrees. If one system is slowed or not working, other systems have to compensate and work over time as they try to maintain homeostasis. A physical organ system can be significantly affected because of a disruption or irregularity of another.

Each of the following bodily organ systems can be impacted by either the physical body or the literal body being out of alignment. Please don't think of these as independent, stand-alone systems, functioning separately from one another. Rather, keep clearly in mind that although each system has a primary function, each impacts and affects all of the others. Learning how to recognize these disruptions and determine the source of the problem is possible, but you must learn how to listen, to use your intuitive self. Logic and intelligence will fail you. With daily practice of Source Connection Therapy you will be able to hear what your body needs to reestablish a strong, positive connection and bring self and Source into harmony.

The following list might remind you of being in junior high school biology class because of its simplicity, but I offer it here just as a reminder of the complexity of the human body. As you read further about the energetic body and the magnificent brain, visualize this list of systems and how they interact. Every system will influence the others.

- **Circulatory system**: pumping and channeling blood to and from the body and lungs with heart, blood, and blood vessels.
- **Digestive system**: digestion and processing food with salivary glands, esophagus, stomach, liver, gallbladder, pancreas, intestines, rectum, and anus.
- **Endocrine system**: communication within the body using hormones made by endocrine glands such as the hypothalamus, pituitary or pituitary gland, pineal body or pineal gland, thyroid, parathyroids and adrenals, i.e., adrenal glands.
- **Integumentary system**: skin, hair, and nails.
- **Lymphatic system**: structures involved in the transfer of lymph between tissues and the blood stream, the lymph and the nodes and vessels that transport it, including the immune system: defending against disease-causing agents with leukocytes, tonsils, adenoids, thymus, and spleen.
- **Muscular system**: movement with muscles.
- **Nervous system**: collecting, transferring, and processing information with brain, spinal cord, peripheral nerves, and nerves.

- **Reproductive system**: the sex organs, such as ovaries, fallopian tubes, uterus, vagina, mammary glands, testes, seminal vesicles, prostate, and penis.

- **Respiratory system**: the organs used for breathing, the pharynx, larynx, trachea, bronchi, lungs, and diaphragm.

- **Skeletal system**: structural support and protection with bones, cartilage, ligaments, and tendons.

- **Urinary system**: kidneys, ureters, bladder, and urethra involved in fluid balance, electrolyte balance, and excretion of urine

Meridians

You should be aware of several common concepts used to describe the energetic body. Primary among these concepts are Meridians. Since the body is generating and utilizing energy, there needs to be a transportation system for this energy to impact all parts of that body. The networks in this transportation system are most commonly referred to as Meridians.

We know for certain that the human body generates electro-magnetic current, or fields of energy. Anyone who has had an electrocardiogram has experienced having electrodes attached to various body parts, from ankles to ribs to chest. Each of these electrodes picks up the heart's electrical pulses and records them on a machine. Similarly, brain waves can be measured by using an electroencephalogram, with electrodes attached to parts of the head that pick up the brain's electrical current. The electro-magnetic fields are there. We can measure them. There is no doubt about that.

We know there is interaction between the heart and brain, and modern science knows that every part of our body is impacted by electro-magnetic fields, either from the heart or brain, or both. Meridians, sometimes referred to as channels, are the systems that move these electrical forces around the body. Imagine a municipal electrical power plant producing electricity. A generating plant by itself is nearly useless. Electricity needs wires, a grid to move from the power plant out to the community. In the human body, that grid is the Meridians. From the source of the electro-magnetic field, the Meridians form the networks to move those forces around and to service the major organs and systems of the body.

Centuries-old Asian medicine has utilized the Meridians for diagnosis and treatment. In fact, along each Meridian lie acupuncture or acupressure points. The myriad points along each Meridian are thought of as connection points within the energy transportation system where pressure or a needle can stimulate a release or redistribution of electro-magnetic energy. Using modern MRI imaging, scientists have conclusively shown that stimulation of certain acupuncture points activates portions of the brain, even when there is no direct physical link between the point and the brain. Donna Eden, for example, describes a commonly used acupuncture point on the toe which stimulates a portion of the brain to which there is no recognized anatomical pathway from that toe. [Eden, 111].

Further scientific evidence that the electro-magnetic fields exist and are influenced either positively or negatively by mental and emotional states is found by examining the points along meridians used by acupuncturists. As with other electro-magnetic fields of the body, testing to verify the subtle energies and energetic impacts of acupuncture points along Meridians is routinely done. Dr. Gerber describes it this way:

> "The acupuncture points along the superficial meridians in the skin demonstrate unique electrical properties, which distinguish them from the surrounding epidermis. The electrical resistance measured in the skin overlying the acupoints is lower than the surrounding skin by a factor of approximately 10 to 1. The value of this resistance, as measured by a special direct current (DC) electrical amplifier, shows that the electrical parameters of the acupuncture points vary according to physiological and emotional changes within the organism." [Gerber, 178].

There are fourteen recognized Meridians, twelve of which are named for organs or the systems they service. The remaining two are the Central Meridian and the Governing Meridian. The Central Meridian runs from the base of the pubic bone to the center of the lower lip, forming a straight line up the front of the body. The Governing Meridian forms a corresponding line on the back, starting at the base of the spine, running straight up the back to the center of the neck and over the head, ending just below the nose. Some experts believe that the Central and Governing Meridians meet behind the throat, rather than on the face.

The Central Meridian (sometimes called the Conception Meridian), running up the front of the body, connects all of the main Chakras and is critical in opening and balancing these Chakras. The Governing Meridian works with the central nervous system, the dural tube, and stimulates production and adsorption of cranial spinal fluid to bathe our cranial nerves. Problems in posture and not standing erect can sometimes be traced to these two Meridians.

The remaining twelve major Meridians are the following:

- **Spleen Meridian**: Regulates digestion, helps control flow of blood in the vessels, affects muscle and limb tone. The Spleen Meridian, if out of balance, can cause general fatigue, abdominal problems, lack of appetite, prolapsed internal organs and weak muscles.

- **Heart Meridian:** Centered on the heart which, of course, pumps blood and oxygen throughout the body, the Heart Meridian is critical and central in maintaining health. A blocked or unbalanced Heart Meridian can show up as heart palpitations, short and shallow breathing, chest pains, dizziness, irritability, difficulty regulating body temperature as well as sleeping problems.

- **Small Intestine Meridian:** Receives food from the stomach, extracts nourishment and passes on the waste material to the large intestine. The small intestine also passes nourishment to the body. Abdominal distension, poor digestion, neuralgia, acne, swollen lymph glands, sore or stiff shoulders, poor circulation with weakness in the legs and feelings of being cold can result from an unbalanced Small Intestine Meridian.

- **Bladder Meridian**: Because the bladder's job is to excrete liquid waste from the body, problems with this Meridian often are reflected in urinary diseases. Shoulder and neck stiffness and back pain can be related to a blocked or unbalanced Bladder Meridian. Headaches are sometimes traced to problems with this meridian.

- **Kidney Meridian**: This meridian is important for regulating overall balance of the body, but specifically relate to the production of bone marrow and blood. In addition, the kidneys are critical in the growth and development of reproductive functions. Difficulties resulting from kidney issues include back pain, genital-urinary problems, asthma, and tinnitus. Willpower and the ability to cope with life are emotional conditions influenced by this meridian.

- **Pericardium**: For energy medicine, the Pericardium is important to understand because it removes excess energy from the heart and moves it outward to the palms of the hands where it dissipates. Also commonly referred to as the **Circulation-Sex Meridian**.
- **Triple Warmer Meridian**: Unlike the other meridians, the Triple Warmer is not associated with a particular organ or organ function; rather, it related to the concept of metabolism. It controls the body's heat and moisture functions and each area influenced by one of the three warmers involves several organs and body systems. As such, the Triple Warmer Meridian could be involved in any disorder, but often will cause hearing problems, fatigue, breathing difficulties, and urinary problems.
- **Gallbladder Meridian**: Helps digest food and stores bile, which is produced by the liver. The Liver Meridian is associated with the Gallbladder Meridian. Pain in the joints, headaches, abdominal symptoms, and back pain are a few of the maladies that can be treated through points on this meridian.
- **Lung Meridian**: Emotionally, the Lung Meridian is associated with sensitivity and the ability to grieve and to make connections with the world around us. Respiration opens the body to infection from outside, such as colds and flu. Abnormal sweating, difficulty in smelling and other problems with the nose are related to the lungs. Liquid is distributed to the skin as a result of metabolic action that the lungs influence; thus, any skin problems, including eczema and psoriasis may be cured by correcting inbalances and blockages in the Lung Meridian.
- **Liver Meridian**: This meridian is extremely important because of its relation to the liver. Menstruation, female sexual cycles, and flexibility are impacted. Illness and physical problems associated with the liver include PMS, jaundice, still joints, vertigo, blurred vision, and headaches.
- **Stomach Meridian**: Worry and nervousness are influenced by the Stomach Meridian. Because the stomach handles digestion, all digestive related problems can be caused by this meridian.
- **Large Intestine Meridian**: Any abdominal pain may be traced

to this meridian. Water from waste material is extracted and passed as solid matter by the large intestine.

As you do Source Connection Therapy on yourself or on others, you should be aware that each of these Meridians impacts at least one major organ and recognize that the combined effect is to service all of the major organs and systems in the body. For our purposes, you don't need to memorize them or know the details of what each does. You will notice, however, that as you do the holds described in later chapters, each combination forms a line that crosses the center of the body. Each of these holds crosses the Central Meridian and the Governing Meridian. This is important because we are reminding the body to make connections of the electro-magnetic fields from left to right sides and from right to left sides, incorporating in each the Central and Governing Meridians. If you want to dig deeper into the study of Meridians, consult the reading list I provide at the end of this book. There are several excellent sources of information, but I find Donna Eden's *Energy Medicine* to be among the most thorough and understandable.

The Meridians connect and impact all the major organs and systems in the human body. The acupuncture points along the Meridians are on the skin, which leads some people to think of the Meridians as running along the surface. The opposite is true. Each Meridian penetrates from the surface to deep within the body and includes the organs along its path. Thus, when doing the Source Connection Therapy holds, I want you to visualize when making a connection between two points crossing the Central and Governing Meridians, that even though your hands are on the surface (touching the skin), the impact of making that connection goes deep into the body and affects the electro-magnetic energy fields of all of the organs, muscles, and tissue along the connection line. You will be awakening the electro-magnetic energy fields throughout the body as you progress through the full treatment therapy and calmly move from one set of holds to another.

When all of the Meridian energy is in balance, the body's organs, systems, and structure are smoothly working together. Electro-magnetic energy throughout the body is aligned, forming smooth, positive fields with steady frequencies. For total wellness and wellbeing, all of the body's systems must be in balance with all of the others.

If, however, any Meridian's energy is weak, the full system will be out of balance. The organ or organs that it services will be at risk of illness. Unbalanced Meridians often precede illness, indicating the organs associated with the Meridian are having problems. Proven methods of checking the body's Meridians can tell us a great deal, even predicting health vulnerabilities. Correcting these out of balance Meridians through a variety of therapies, including Source Connection Therapy, often can prevent disease and illness.

To balance Meridian energy is to get it running smoothly and efficiently. The Meridian balance can be achieved in several ways, each of which is based on the fact that the body has its own ability to correct out of balance Meridians. Many forget that our bodies sometimes need a reminder through the guidance and healing atmosphere created by therapy. Years of experience tells us, after all, that the body knows what it needs, and that it will not lie. The body will tell us what it needs, but we must listen carefully and correctly. Our minds, however, will tell us all sorts of things, most frequently deceiving us, and can't be trusted in these matters. Only when the mind and body are connected properly does true healing begin. We humans are, after all, instinctual beings. We just need to rely on those instincts to understand what truly is going on within ourselves. That reliance will be possible only when we are balanced.

Muscle Energy Testing Before and After SCT

At the start of a Source Connection Therapy training workshop in Seattle, my colleague Cindy Wright, an expert in energy medicine, conducted muscle energy testing on three volunteer students at the workshop. Muscle energy testing is an integral part of evaluating clients for treatment in Cindy's practice. We wanted to see if there was an improvement in the out of balance meridians resulting from Source Connection Therapy treatment.

Before the treatment, Cindy found the following:

Volunteer #1: Her governing meridian, bladder meridian, and kidney meridian were all weak.

Volunteer #2: Her large intestine meridian was weak.

Volunteer #3: Her stomach, gallbladder, liver, and spleen meridians were all weak.

> After Source Connection Therapy treatment, all
> of the identified meridian weaknesses of each of the
> three volunteers had been balanced. We were happy to
> report that after an hour session, all of the meridians
> were balanced and functioning at full capacity. Cindy
> uses Source Connection Therapy as a regular part of her
> treatment protocol with her clients. She sees positive
> results with every session.

Source Connection Therapy, among several therapies including acupuncture, is an effective way of balancing the Meridians. A widely accepted method of testing the effectiveness of a therapy in correcting Meridian balance is to conduct muscle energy testing. This testing method checks the integrity of the Meridians. By conducting muscle energy testing prior to a Source Connection Therapy session and again immediately after a thirty- to sixty-minute treatment, we have quite consistently seen that previously out of balance Meridians are well balanced as a result of Source Connection Therapy.

Chakras

The term Chakra is translated to mean disk or vortex. Some define Chakra as a station or location of energy. In relation to the energetic body, these Chakras can be thought of as the tree of life's center, its core. The Chakras are energy vortexes located at specific parts of the body, each of which can affect the total wellbeing of the body. The Chakras impact the physical, psychological, and spiritual aspects of our lives.

Physically, the Chakras, as stations of energy, surround and nurture the organs near them with that energy. This energy protection is crucial to the health of that organ or system. The shape and function of Chakras has been explained in a variety of ways, but most frequently writers describe the Chakra as a location on the body over which energy spins, like a vortex. Although the Chakras are most often described as being like little tornadoes over the area of the body they influence, it is very important to realize that the influence of each Chakra penetrates deep into the body, encompassing the associated organs and systems.

As they pertain to psychological aspects of life, the Chakras will influence and be influenced by "survival and sexuality (root chakra), creativity (womb chakra), identity and power (solar plexus chakra), love and compassion (heart chakra), expression (throat chakra), deep perception and understanding (third eye chakra), and transcendence of self (crown chakra)." [Eden, 149-50].

Information, such as your history, is thought to be coded in the Chakras and to impact spiritual functions.

When the Chakras are functioning properly, they are described as being smooth appearing, consistent in color, and extending fully from front to back of the person. An out of balance or damaged Chakra is often described as appearing torn. When all Chakras are in harmony, the person's core is strong and well-grounded. Energy not only moves in through the Chakras, but will be passed on to the body and its various systems as outgoing secondary energies. The Chakras are critical locations of energy for our bodily system, but also are the energy vortexes that send our energy outward to Source and to our environment.

The seven primary Chakras, energy stations, include the following, described in the order you would see them in the body: [See Illustration 3-2: page 37]

- **Root Chakra** – Associated with autonomic functioning of the body, such as breathing and heart function. This Chakra affects stimulation and controlling structures not under conscious control.

- **Sacral Chakra** – In general, this Chakra is involved with the emotional parts of our beings. It is also referred to as the womb and creativity Chakra.

- **Solar Plexus Chakra** – Associated with mental processes, as opposed to emotional aspects of life. This Chakra is the vortex of linear thinking.

- **Heart Chakra** – The fourth level of Chakras is the conduit through which we feel love, both on a personal level such as a mate, but on a broader level such as love of humanity.

- **Throat Chakra** – This Chakra is the power of our words. It is the center associated with our voice and the power of voices speaking the truth, encompassing listening and being responsible for our own actions.

- **Pituitary (Third Eye) Chakra** – Seeing beyond what is apparent and bringing that knowledge into balance with our physical beings is the essence of this Chakra. One may think of this Chakra as our intuition.

- **Crown Chakra** – This Chakra is the direct line to Source (God). It is through this Chakra that we are enabled to hear what we need for our highest good. Opening this Chakra reunites left and right cerebral hemispheres for achieving maximum mental capacity.

Other writers have described in detail a larger number of layers of auras and Chakras. For the purposes of Source Connection Therapy, we will limit our discussion to these major seven. Realize, however, that all energetic and physical functions are positively affected by Source Connection Therapy.

There are specific locations within our energy system for sensations, emotions, thoughts, memories, and other nonphysical experiences. If any or all of these systems are out of balance, then we will be steered in directions that will not be beneficial for our health and happiness.

Each level of Chakra has its own function, and they are all of equal importance. Consider, however, that if any one of the Chakras is out of balance with the others, the person will have a sense of not being organized, of being unsafe, or having a loss of direction. Most often, people suffering from this imbalance tell me they feel *out of sorts*. The Root Chakra, for example, is a person's core, or base. Just like in martial arts, if the opponent's base can be knocked off balance, that person becomes vulnerable. In life, if the Root Chakra is out of balance, all other Chakras will be affected and most, if not all aspects of life will suffer.

While applying Source Connection Therapy on yourself or on others, you will notice that the connection holds you apply cross the center line of the body, most passing directly through the location of the Chakras. Source Connection Therapy reminds these Chakras to expand their energies, to reconnect vital functions within the body. The Chakras awaken and so does the energy transportation system of the Meridians.

Energy is heightened and all organs and systems are positively impacted. Physical, mental, and spiritual balance are attained.

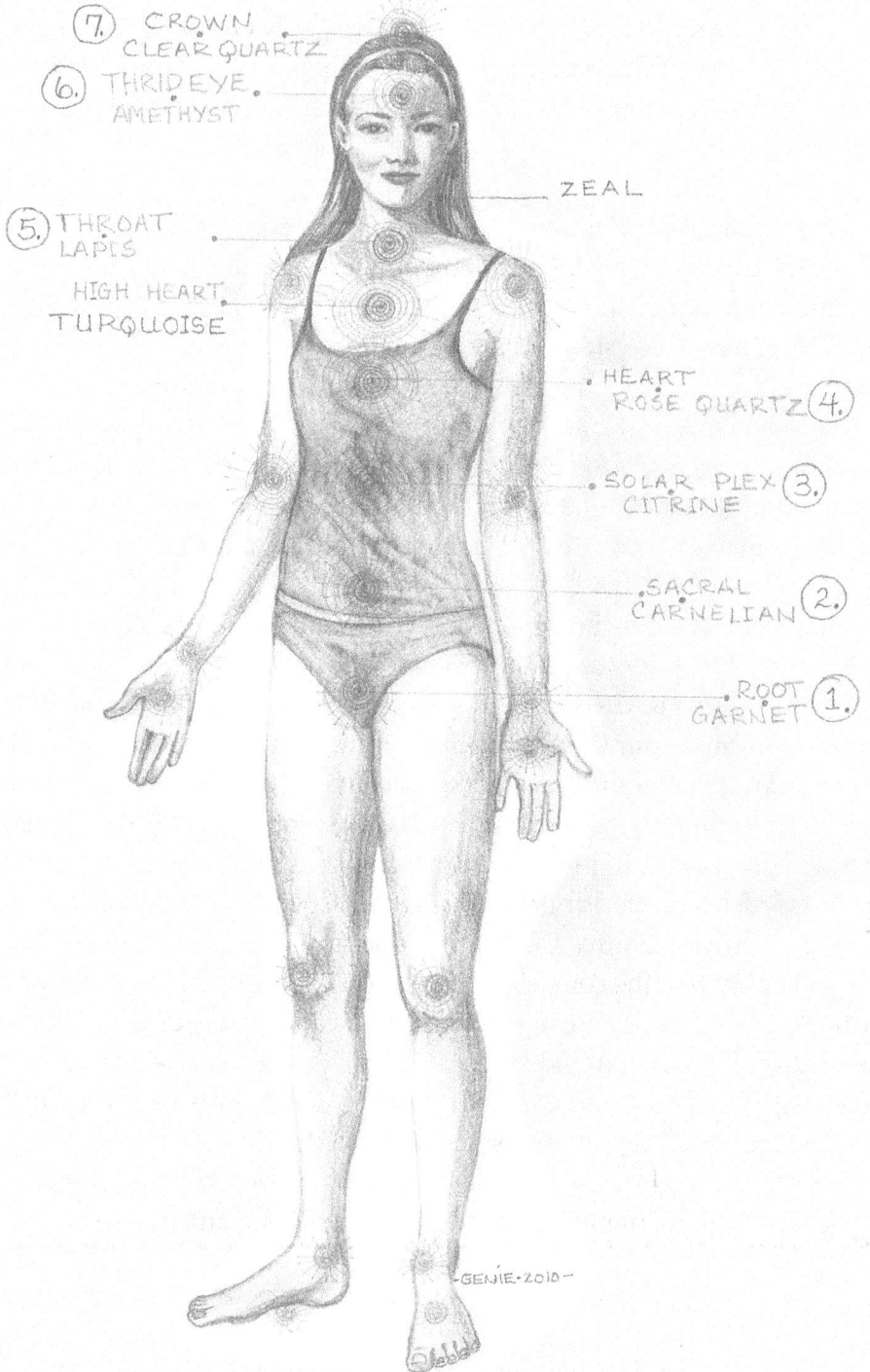

Illust. 3-2. Seven primary Chakras.

$\heartsuit$

Chapter 4
The Body Mind Connection

Brain Hemispheres

$\mathcal{W}$riters on the topic of the energetic body too often fail to include a significant aspect of our energy systems: the left and right brain hemispheres. Because our physical, mental, and emotional lives are so complicated and require a great deal of specialization, describing the Meridians and Chakras may not sufficiently explain the full impact of balancing the whole person. Through Source Connection Therapy, you will not only be bringing the energetic body into balance, but you also will be opening the connection between the left and right cerebral hemispheres, bringing them back into ideal harmony with one another and balancing them with the other systems of the body.

I know I don't have to tell you this, but here goes anyway: The brain is a very complicated thing, and we don't know much about how it works or its limitations. There, I said it. If you want to learn more, check out the reading list at the end of this book. For our purposes here, there are some specifics that apply to Source Connection Therapy that we do need to examine a bit. In relation to the energetic body, I think it's significant that we understand the basic functioning of the two cerebral hemispheres and how they work together, or fail to work together. In addition, there are some more subtle but important aspects of brain function that will either promote or inhibit our ability to learn, communicate, and be open to Source.

Certain discussions get a little confused unless we distinguish between the brain as an organ of the body, and the mind as the operation of that organ. The term *brain* refers to the physical thing inside your skull. The term *mind* refers to the functioning of that brain, especially as it applies to promoting learning, health, and healing.

The left side of your brain controls the right side of your body and vice versa. A physical problem encountered on the left side of your body could relate to an issue involving the right brain hemisphere. This cross-over of function from right brain to left body control, and details of what the left and right sides of your brain do, is not related to being left or right handed.

Obviously, our mind receives and processes huge amounts of information. It allows us to learn and to reason through problems. Our mind interprets the environment around us, sends alarms when there is trouble, and makes us feel safe when it senses security. Our mind can dream and influences the health of our physical bodies. Yet our mind also can block learning and stop effective communication.

The limbic system functions in a very unique way, placing values and emotions on the stimuli our minds receive. Our central nervous system receives information and inputs data, sending it toward the cerebral cortex for processing. Before these data reach the cerebral cortex, however, the limbic system attaches emotions, giving the data an effect it would otherwise not have. Fear, anger, rage, and similar negative emotions will be attached in situations where we are uncomfortable, sense danger, or feel pain. In unfamiliar, uncomfortable circumstances the limbic system will focus on the negative and interfere with our ability to learn. Where the limbic system has attached rage or anger or intense fear to an input, we may become incapable of handling any new information at all.

Without the limbic system's interference, we would be creatures stuck in a logical world without emotion. All information we receive would be neutral, representing just the facts. How boring that would be. What dull lives we would lead if it were not for our emotions.

With Source Connection Therapy, the limbic system comes into play in two very important ways:

First, not only can the limbic system render learning difficult, if not impossible, it can interfere in the opening of the Crown Chakra, making communication with Source impossible. A significant aspect of Source Connection Therapy is the full balancing of the body, mind, and spirit, looking toward the final goal of hearing the messages from Source.

If your mind is in a state of anger or fear, or even just unsettled because of uncomfortable conditions, most therapies will be ineffective. With

Source Connection Therapy, though, this is exactly what we are balancing. In fact, balancing with Source Connection Therapy will settle the fear or anger, bringing you back to a calmer state.

Second, if you try to balance another person using Source Connection Therapy while you are in an unbalanced state, I believe you will fail. If you feel uncomfortable or are angry, for example, you likely will be unable to help another person effectively. You may pass these negative emotions on to the person with whom you are applying the Source Connection Therapy protocol, fully defeating the purpose of the therapy. Balance yourself, then help others.

To prevent the negative states of mind resulting from emotions such as fear and anger, I strongly recommend to all my clients, and I practice it myself daily, to find a quiet setting, away from negative distractions. Then, lie down or sit and relax for a bit, calming your nerves, smoothing out your emotions, and begin focusing inward. Block out noise around you, maybe using earphones and listen to soothing music if that helps. Allow your muscles to relax and your mind to wander a bit. Visualize being in a comfortable place, safe from all outside influences.

An important aspect of meditation is the relaxation of the body and the focusing of the mind in such a manner that the limbic system calms and opens channels for learning and listening. I realize there are times when you feel a need to balance yourself, but can't be in a place that's perfectly suited. In these situations, do the best you can and let your imagination help you visualize a peaceful setting. Don't try this if it will distract you, but I've balanced myself while driving on a long road trip.

At health fairs, I've balanced clients under bright lights, in noisy rooms full of bustling people. Even where there are a number of distractions, the balancing through Source Connection Therapy can work, where other modalities fail.

Apply the same concept when you're working with another person. It's important that both of you be in a positive, calm state of mind in order to gain the maximum benefits from Source Connection Therapy. By achieving this calm, comfortable, safe mental state, your limbic system will not only stop interfering with your progress, but will actually open your mind to better learning and listening. Your connection with Source will be more open and more direct when you approach the therapy in a calm manner with a clear mind and open Crown Chakra.

The general rule about brain hemispheres is that left brain is logical and has memory, voice, and can do math. The right brain lives in the moment and is the center of artistic talents. Left brain is the responsible, logical one that stores your history and allows you to think of the future. The right brain is less responsible, more prone to aesthetics than logic and has no memory and sees no future. The two hemispheres are connected by *corpus callosum* forming a pathway for information transfer between the two hemispheres. The two hemispheres *think* differently and in different ways, but when they are balanced, they complement one another so perfectly we don't even realize our brains are two distinct parts. We reach our highest level of mental achievement when the two sides are working in perfect balance.

This definition of left and right brain functions is a vast over simplification because there are variations among different people's brains. Some, for example, have the verbal center in left brain, while with others it's located in the right brain. Even though it's a simplification, the general rule that right is artistic and the left is logical is useful to us in analyzing life-styles and corresponding physical, mental, and emotional issues. With Source Connection Therapy we progress through levels of energy balancing until we reach a point at which we are helping realign and rejoin the two hemispheres.

Often without you even knowing it, the two hemispheres can move out of alignment, out of balance. Inactivity, disease, stroke, stress, or injury can, to varying degrees, disrupt the free flow of information through the *corpus callosum*. These ill effects also can cause one hemisphere to reduce or lose function. In severe cases, such as a stroke, a person can lose total function of one of the hemispheres.

With mild situations of minor imbalance between the left and right brains, you can still function—walk, talk, and take care of yourself—but still not be at your maximum potential. In these instances, balancing through Source Connection Therapy will revive the energy throughout your body and bring the two hemispheres into sync, promoting wellness and wellbeing.

As I mentioned in the previous chapter, one of the most remarkable books I have read dealing with the brain is Dr. Taylor's *My Stroke of Insight.* I recommend this book to you without hesitation. Dr. Taylor's stroke resulted in the loss of her left brain, the most extreme imbalance possible. In her situation, Dr. Taylor describes in the clearest detail just how different and how remarkable the two brain hemispheres are.

The onset of symptoms caused by a severe stroke were centered in her left brain hemisphere, and she became aware of functions shutting down. Most remarkable to me is that her right-side brain function was taking control and blocking her from the terror that otherwise would have overcome her. Her left brain was quitting and her right brain was telling her to relax and enjoy not having to deal with the reality that is the practical, logical side of her thinking.

The verbal side of Dr. Taylor's mind was quitting and the right side began showing images, snapshot photos of the moments as they passed, removing any history or future from her thoughts. Analytical brain activity was fading, taking with it her ability to use language, to understand dimensions of herself, and to work through the problems she suddenly faced.

Because her description so succinctly shows what can happen when the two sides of the brain quit cooperating, I am taking the liberty of quoting quite lengthy selected passages from her book:

> "In that instant, I suddenly felt vulnerable, and I noticed that the constant brain chatter that routinely familiarized me with my surroundings was no longer a predictable and constant flow of conversation. Instead, my verbal thoughts were inconsistent, fragmented, and interrupted by an intermittent silence.

> ". . . As my brain chatter began to disintegrate, I felt an odd sense of isolation. My blood pressure must have been dropping as a result of the bleeding in my brain because I felt as if all of my systems, including my mind's ability to instigate movement, were moving into a slow mode of operation. Yet, even though my thoughts were no longer a constant stream of chatter about the external world and my relationship to it, I was conscious and constantly present within my mind.

> "The harder I tried to concentrate, the more fleeting my ideas seemed to be. Instead of finding answers and information, I met a growing sense of peace. In place of that constant chatter that had attached me to the details of my life, I felt enfolded by a blanket of tranquil euphoria. How fortunate I was that the portion of my brain that registered fear, my amygdale, had not reacted with alarm to these unusual circumstances and shifted me into a state of panic... In this

void of higher cognition and details pertaining to my normal life, my consciousness soared into an all-knowingness, a *being at one* with the universe, if you will. In a compelling sort of way, it felt like the good road home and I liked it.

"My body was propped up against the shower wall, and I found it odd that I was aware that I could no longer clearly discern the physical boundaries of where I began and where I ended. I sensed the composition of my being as that of a fluid rather than that of a solid. I no longer perceived myself as a whole object separate from everything. Instead, I now blended in with the space and flow around me. Beholding a growing sense of detachment between my cognitive mind and my ability to control and finely manipulate my fingers, the mass of my body felt heavy and my energy waned.

". . . In this altered state of being, my mind was no longer preoccupied with the billions of details that my brain routinely used to define and conduct my life in the external world. Those little voices, that brain chatter that customarily kept me abreast of myself in relation to the world outside of me, were delightfully silent. And in their absence, my memories of the past and my dreams of the future evaporated. I was alone. In the moment, I was alone with nothing but the rhythmic pulse of my beating heart." [Taylor, 40-43].

Obviously, Dr. Taylor's situation was extreme and far beyond what we normally see when using Source Connection Therapy, but it shows several relevant things. One is that we can't trust our brains to tell us what our bodies need. Even though Dr. Taylor was in desperate trouble with serious bleeding in her left brain, her mind kept telling her it would be okay, that this feeling of euphoria is actually a good thing. Second, her story warns us that if our two brain hemispheres are out of sync, the impacts may be so subtle that we don't even recognize it.

Both sides of our brains need exercise to function properly and in cooperation with one another. Research and experience with programs such as the Brain Gym (educational kinesiology) are finding that physical movement can enhance brain function. In discussions with people who work with young children who have learning or attention problems, as well as with elderly patients suffering dementia, we learn that physical activities that cross the mid-line of the body bring brain hemispheres together, with very beneficial results. I believe the cross-body work with

Source Connection Therapy has a similar benefit, not only bringing the two brain hemispheres together, but also uniting body and mind.

A person whose job becomes all consuming, one that demands a great deal of focus, detailed work, and disciplined logic may actually be neglecting the right brain, forcing a slight imbalance.

She Forgot She Had a Body

A twenty-seven-year-old Law student was studying to take the bar exam after working herself through law school. As the date of the exam drew near, her focus became so directed at the study material that her lifestyle changed without her recognizing it. Without realizing how drastically her daily patterns had changed, she became totally engrossed in the effort to pass this test. Her health deteriorated simply because she wasn't taking care of herself as she normally would.

She ignored symptoms such as fatigue and irritability until she began having panic attacks. These attacks were so serious and so frightening that on two occasions, she went to the hospital. The doctors inquired about her life and concluded that the issue clearly was a panic attack. After she explained she was studying to take the state bar exam, to the doctors' credit, not one of them suggested medication. In each case, the physicians talked with her about her symptoms possibly being stress related.

Under pressure of the deadline, her lifestyle changed and she developed unhealthy patterns. She didn't eat well, drank too much coffee, and was sleep deprived from studying late into the night, every night. Her brain was so engaged with left-brain subjects that the right brain became inactive. She clearly was out of balance physically and mentally. As this unhealthy pattern continued, her body started reacting, sending out cries for help. Her literal body was asking her to take care of it. She was so dedicated to the exam, that she wasn't even aware of her declining health situation.

Having been ignored, her literal body reacted. She experienced frequent shaking. Breathing became difficult and irregular, and she often felt heart palpitations. Finally, when her body couldn't handle it any longer, it basically started giving out. Escalating panic attacks provided a wake up call, forcing her to seek professional help.

After consulting with doctors, she called me on the phone and we did balancing with Source Connection Therapy. We worked together to get her more balanced, bringing her right brain back on line and reuniting the two brain hemispheres. She said she felt better almost instantly after the balancing treatment. After that, we did daily balancing sessions over the telephone since we live in different parts of the country.

Yes, she passed the bar exam on the first try.

Even a slight imbalance between the hemispheres can cause a person to function far below par and can lead to even more serious health problems, including mental and emotional issues. Stress inhibits the connections between right and left brain hemispheres. Successful brain function requires complete connections across the neural pathways located throughout the brain. The lateral relationship between the two sides of the brain, especially mid-field where the two sides must integrate, is critical for specialty skills such as reading, writing, listening, or speaking.

The relationship between right and left brain—their ability to communicate with one another—is essential for patterning whole body movement as well as being able to move and think at the same time.

The front and rear of our brains are about comprehension, the ability to blend, including context and detail focus. The top and bottom of the brain form the connection for emotion and rational thought.

Finding weakness in meridian energy or a disruption of the electro-magnetic energy fields along one side of the body can indicate several problems, one of which can relate to the opposite side brain hemisphere. During later phases of Source Connection Therapy protocol, you'll bring the two hemispheres into alignment. In doing so, you'll open the Crown Chakra and build a strong connection to your higher self and your Source.

Listening to Our Literal Bodies

Fundamental to understanding and succeeding with Source Connection Therapy is the concept that you must learn to listen to your body and understand the meaning of its messages. Each person's body is sending messages all the time. Our bodies tell us of joy, pain, or unease.

Some of these messages sent by our physical bodies are easy to hear, even being unavoidable, such as the pain one feels when touching a hot skillet. Other messages, however, are quite subtle and extremely difficult to see or hear. A growing sense of depression, for example, may trigger a physical symptom that warns us of deeper issues. Take the time to listen and understand.

Our bodies are, of course, physical and can send us messages such as suffering pain from a physical injury. But, our bodies also are literal, which can result in physical problems caused by mental and emotional stresses.

Your literal body is constantly sending you messages. Life burdens, being over worked, living under constant stress are examples of conditions that could be related to a physical complaint, which I see as a message from your literal body.

Here are some examples to show what I mean by the literal body. Chronic fatigue, fibromyalgia symptoms, and frozen shoulder are serious health issues for which modern medicine has not determined a cause. In fact, fibromyalgia is classified as a syndrome, which means it has a group of signs or characteristics that occur simultaneously, including intense pain in various places around the body. Problems with muscles, connective tissues, joints, and a host of other symptoms affect more than six-million people in the United States. Are these symptoms actually messages from the body telling us we are doing too much, living out of balance? Reports indicate that most often people suffering these symptoms are Type A personalities who push themselves hard.

I'm not saying that Source Connection Therapy will cure fibromyalgia or similar problems. Also, I'm not saying these syndromes aren't real; rather, I work on people all the time who have these symptoms, which are very genuine.

In my practice, I encounter clients with these combined syndromes and individual symptoms almost daily. Because of that intense experience working with these clients, I'm suggesting these syndromes may simply be the body telling you that it's time to change paths, slow down, and pay attention to what your body needs. It may be time to change your diet and exercise, or learn to meditate or pray. These syndromes may be your literal body shutting down because you didn't listen.

When I work on clients with fibromyalgia symptoms and similar complaints, I'm acutely aware they are suffering. I also am aware the symptoms that various clients express vary widely and do not appear to be degenerative, which is unusual if this were a true disease.

Cellular or tissue memory is well accepted as a potential physical manifestation that may have a non-physical cause. Somatization disorder is a condition with a psychological cause and physical symptoms. With Somatization disorder, doctors are unable to identify a physical cause for the condition. The symptoms are most often pain or discomfort of some type that may last for years. A traumatic experience can cause energy to enter the physical body systems where it remains because cells and soft tissue have a memory. If this memory isn't broken and the energy released, the pain or physical manifestations can increase in severity and become chronic. Through specific and repeated touch therapies, these physical manifestations can be released from the client's tissue, resulting in a reduction in pain and enhanced wellness. With Source Connection Therapy I'm finding similar, positive results with clients who are experiencing pain without an identified medical cause.

In my work I also notice a wide range of symptoms, such as depression and sleep disorders. They can happen to anyone when not dealing adequately with life's stresses. When you are overwhelmed and worried, many of the symptoms described by my clients will slow you down and can even cause debilitation.

So, let's take a look at some of the symptoms, and let me explain how they relate to the concept of the literal body and why it is so important to listen and pay attention to what your body is telling you. There are so many situations we can relate this to, where our autoimmune system is compromised. I use these examples here because so many of my clients have suffered from them. I also mention these specific symptoms because clients and I, working together, have achieved success in reducing or eliminating these problems. This success is especially true for those clients who changed their lifestyles.

Pick any day you have twenty to fifty things you think you have to get done in a single day, then check with yourself and see if that isn't the day you locked your keys in your car, forgot the most important thing on your list, or even ran a stop sign. These are common symptoms of being out of balance. These are signals from your literal self telling you to slow down, take a deep breath, and get a grip. This is the time to listen to your literal body and take the time to balance. Source Connection Therapy can start your recovery.

Study a list of overlapping conditions associated with fibromyalgia and ask yourself if these are things that happened to you during times of extreme stress or when there was just too much to do. As I look at these symptoms and talk with clients during treatment, here are some of the conclusions I've reached about each of them. I chose this list because these are perfect examples of letting the body go to the breaking point.

- **Chronic fatigue**: This is the literal body telling you that you have done too much. You are worn out, exhausted. My advice is simply to rest. Take time away from the things causing stress, even if it is just for a few minutes. Give yourself a break.

- **Irritable bowel**: Eating on the run, not relaxing so your body can properly digest its fuel. You may not be allowing time enough for you to *digest life*. Living in such a stressful state that your bodily systems are out of balance can cause anyone to have these problems. Become aware of what your body is telling you. Watch what you eat and how you eat. Make sure your food is giving you nutrition. Avoid excessive amounts of caffeine and sodas (especially diet soft drinks). See if your eating habits are a symptom of not taking in life joyously. Take the time to be responsible for yourself. Answer the calls from your literal body.

- **Temporomandibular joint syndrome (TMJ)**: This is damage to the joint of your jaw that causes pain, makes chewing difficult, and results in snapping and popping noises when you move your jaw. In some cases, this is caused by an accident. Excessive gum chewers often feel similar pain. Being in the dentists' chair for a long time can cause the same feeling, but in serious cases, the long-lasting pain of TMJ is caused from clenching teeth or even grinding teeth during sleep. Often I find that clients with this problem are holding back from asserting their voices. They are in difficult situations at work or at home and are unable to express those concerns. They tighten their jaws, holding back their feelings and their words. After a long time, the jaw joint wears down and the problem becomes one for the physical body. The solution, obviously, is to overcome the issues that are causing the jaw clenching. Talk things out with a friend or counselor. Take time to relax and try to think through all of the issues in life that are causing this tension.

- **Multiple chemical sensitivities**: This includes situations where a person becomes unexpectedly sensitive to chemicals which otherwise did not cause problems, such as perfume, cleaning products, or materials at work. Again, the reactions are not typical of disease because they differ so widely among people. The most common reactions are headaches, fatigue, dizziness, nausea, memory problems, breathing problems, and feeling flu-like symptoms with rashes and hives. Medical researchers are actively looking into the syndrome, but don't yet understand it.

- My feeling is, these are signs of autoimmune failures caused from *one more stress pushing us over the edge.* Exposing yourself daily to more and more chemicals in the environment and driving yourself too hard can cause this syndrome. Again, you need to take responsibility for yourself, including eating wholesome food and using caution to avoid the unbelievable cocktail of chemicals you may be exposed to every day.

- **Restless leg syndrome**: Many people who are diagnosed with fibromyalgia have feelings of creeping, crawling, and tugging feelings in their legs when they lie down to fall asleep. The sensations start when you try to relax. Doctors say RLS is a neurological condition, but they don't yet know what causes it. In my experience, these symptoms appear closely related to muscle spasms. Some of my clients have solved RLS problems simply by taking the time to change their diets, especially making a dramatic reduction of salt. I suggest that my clients with these types of symptoms slow down and listen to their literal bodies. One of my clients who is now completely free of RLS symptoms said it is not caused by neurological problems; rather, she said, "It was salt interacting with other chemicals in my body. After putting up with RLS and swollen ankles for twenty years, I was able to completely cure myself by balancing and improving my diet. My body was trying to tell me I was not treating it correctly, and I finally listened."

Left unattended, these literal body issues can lead to unhealthy patterns such as long-standing strains, chronic pain, depression, and fatigue. Even a physical injury that is not healing properly may be related to a literal body issue. In my practice, I often find that the failure of a client's body to heal presents a pathway toward a deeper understanding of their actual injury. Often, that injury is related to the literal body such as disruption in the electro-magnetic field, the Meridians, or the Chakras. Any of these energetic body aspects being out of balance can cause an injury to not heal or will manifest in ways that are difficult to understand.

Often, if unattended these literal body issues can result in terminal illness as well as the syndromes described above. The continual breakdown of the body's balance points (not flushing toxin properly, not paying attention to life's stresses, and not coming up with adequate ways of dealing with problems) can have disastrous results. Not all cancer results from literal body issues, but I firmly believe that much of it does. A person who hates herself or her body may end up with a life-threatening cancer, which may have been avoided or cured through early detection had she paid attention to her literal body. Paying attention to Source, loving yourself, and doing what is necessary to live a meaningful, joyful life are key.

The health issues I briefly discussed here are but a fraction of the problems you can face if you ignore the signs and messages. But, for a large number of these ailments, the answer of where to start healing is the same: be positive, connect with yourself, then connect with Source to find the answers you need to move forward. This book, I hope, gives you a tangible tool to begin your personal path to healing and greater joy.

Serious illness is often just the luck of the draw. People get sick sometimes for reasons totally unexplained. Yet even with these bad situations, we have a choice on how to live our lives. If you chose to listen, to stay balanced, and stay connected with Source, then every day can have meaning and positive fulfillment. A fulfilling, joyous life is possible even under negative circumstances.

A client of mine, for example, was in the final stages of a terminal disease. I worked with her doing therapeutic massage and a Source Connection Therapy treatment every week for the final twelve weeks of her life. She had been treated with chemicals for pancreatic cancer for three years. Even when the chemical treatments failed, she still kept her weekly appointments with me. She often told me she didn't want to miss the balancing with Source Connection Therapy. Whether this client's positive attitude was something she brought to me naturally or if the balancing helped maintain it for her, I can't say for sure. Regardless, I found her spirit and her attitude infectious even near the end of her life. Even as her body failed, her spirit remained high. I believe it was a connection to her Source that carried her through this ordeal and helped keep her balanced. Her energy fields were strong, and they impacted me, just as my balancing therapies helped her. Her spirit reminded me that every day can be the best day ever. That spirit carried her to the end of life with dignity and quality. She was walking with her sisters only three days before she passed away.

The practice of Source Connection Therapy is one of the many ways to achieve this positive, fulfilling, and joyous life. Even a person with terminal illness can enjoy a level of health, mentally and spiritually.

Having covered all of this background information, let's step into your own health and balance. Let's start now, turning to how to do Source Connection Therapy. In the next three chapters I will give you the basics of Source Connection Therapy, guidance on doing the therapy yourself, and then how to share it with friends and family. I'm not promising that Source Connection Therapy will cure cancer. It may not prevent acne or menstrual cramps. This therapy is not guaranteed to solve all your problems, but what it will do is give you the opportunity to change unhealthy habits and establish new, positive habits that will be reflected in your physical, spiritual, and mental health.

Source Connection Therapy will remind you of your body's internal grid, your core structure that will support you physically during tough times as well as good times. It will bring you to a place of personal understanding and responsibility to self. In turn, that understanding and responsibility will be translated to others and the Earth.

Chapter 5
Source Connection Therapy - An Overview

$\mathcal{A}$s we are bombarded by negative or weak energy, our core is weakened because negative energy causes a disruption in the body's electro-magnetic fields. With this disruption, our inner self becomes unbalanced, resulting in the body disassociating, becoming fragmented. In addition, the left and right brain hemispheres no longer communicate with one another in an intelligent way. In other words, the body has become unbalanced, unhealthy. The body wants to be in harmony, it wants to be balanced and healthy, in a state of homeostasis.

Source Connection Therapy reunites naturally-occurring energetic connections in our bodies that are often broken through life's stresses, including emotional, physical, and mental injury. The benefits of restoring these connections include the quieting of the central nervous system and reconnecting the right and left brain hemispheres. The result is relaxation, focus, and a greater ability for the body to heal itself. As we become more aligned with Source, we are able to hear what our bodies need. Following the guidance of this book, one will feel a noticeable improvement in sleep patterns, increased feelings of wellbeing, and an enhanced ability to handle life's ups and downs.

To understand the therapy and gain maximum benefit from it, one should understand it in broader terms. Generally, Source Connection Therapy is a proven method of reminding the body to bring itself into homeostasis—balance and harmony. Through Source Connection Therapy, we can help the body achieve the balance it wants and needs. During the therapy, we are not making the connections ourselves; rather, we are opening the pathway, reminding the body that it can achieve balance and health by connecting the points we touch. In fact, it is possible to make this reminder without actually touching if our thoughts can be focused well enough on the points I discuss later.

Source Connection Therapy—for a professional therapist or for one to apply himself or herself—is a proven way to firm the electro-magnetic fields. Once the electro-magnetic field is cleared and firm, the body has the opportunity to find balance within itself. The brain hemispheres connect and the person becomes balanced.

The protocol includes using one's hands to touch two specific points on the body at a time. Each of these connections crosses the midline of the body. Touching particular places on the body reminds the body of the naturally-occurring connection grid that forms the energetic structure of our bodies.

Touching a point on one side of the body, then a corresponding point on the other side of the body reminds the body to firm up that connection corresponding to particular parts and functions of the energetic being.

For example, the first connection hold I will show goes from the scapula (back of shoulder) to the opposite hip. This particular hold sends an energetic vibration between both of these flat bones, to even out or firm up any weak energy, smoothing and combing the electro-magnetic field. This energy becomes firm and reunites the core structure lying between the two points.

Although all of the holds in this therapy are interrelated and each impacts all the others, it helps to consider the holds as sets forming a layering of benefits. The first layer, or set of holds, sets the stage for your body to heal. This set of holds strengthens connections on the body, clears and firms the electro-magnetic fields. Why does it matter if your electro-magnetic fields are clear and firm? One reason: it opens the connection between Source and Earth. These holds clear the negative, weak energies and protect the body from further negative impacts from outside influences while the remaining connections are made.

When you're clear, you are able to make calm and educated decisions based on the balance between your intuition and intellect during this ever changing life. These holds connect the masculine with the feminine, the front and the back, the brain (thoughts) and heart (emotions). This first set of holds, then, opens the way for connection, protection, and healing. Your body is placed in a receptive state for healing.

The second set, or layer of holds works with the Meridians, the energetic pathways throughout our body. This layer also opens and balances the Chakras, which are centers of energy. In addition, this set of holds will help stimulate your body's physiological systems. During this phase of Source Connection Therapy, connections are made with all the body's systems, such as the respiratory system and the circulatory system, bringing them into balance. For example, the hold between the collar bone and the rib on the opposite side crosses the heart Chakra, the physical heart, the solar plexus, diaphragm, and the other organs, helping to clear any blockages in the Meridians and balancing adjacent Chakras. The importance of opening and balancing the Heart Chakra is that it makes the connection between your physical self and your ethereal self—the spiritual connection and love protection.

The third layer of holds reinforces the connection between your mental and physical selves. This layer of holds helps the body connect the mental with the physical, forming connections between the head and the body. These holds work with the thought processes and how you integrate them and communicate them. You are, in this phase of the protocol, working to help connect your senses with your intuition—connecting how you sense, speak, hear, and see. This phase of the treatment also correlates closely with the craniosacral therapies, helping to realign structures that have been stuck in negative, jammed myofascial strain patterns. This phase of Source Connection Therapy helps balance the craniosacral system.

Once your body makes connections with all three layers, you are brought back into alignment and are once again self-contained. You are no longer tugged about by life's stresses.

Here is a brief description of Myofascial Release and Craniosacral Therapy that I use in my classes:

Myofascial Release (MFR) is a technique that works with our fascial system, which is composed of an elasto-collagenous complex. The fascia is the slightly mobile connective tissue that is derived embryologically from esoderm. The purpose of MFR is to release restrictions within the deeper layers of the fascia.

Functionally, the fascia serves to surround and infuse every structure and, therefore, helps to support and protect the structures. It creates separation between vessels, organs, bones, and muscles. Fascia also creates space through which delicate nerves, blood vessels, and fluid must pass. Fascial complex creates a three-dimensional web that extends continuously from the top of the head to the tip of the toes without interruption.

Fascia has the propensity through trauma, inflammatory processes, and poor posture to become solidified and shortened. Fascia will then organize along the lines of tension imposed upon it. This can create bizarre and seemingly unrelated clinical results in adjacent areas of the body. The loss of fascial mobility produces a drag on the fascial system, which manifests itself as abnormal alterations in the craniosacral physiological motion.

Craniosacral Therapy (CST): The craniosacral system is a semi-closed system comprised of the dural tube, which houses cerebrospinal fluid, the meningeal membranes, the cranial bones, connective tissue structures that are intimately related to meningeal membranes, and all structure related to production, re-absorption, and containment of the cerebrospinal fluid.

A complete craniosacral cycle consists of flexion, extension, and a neutral phase (relaxation). Craniosacral therapy is working with the craniosacral system to help restore mobility and function for a whole-body approach to the treatment of pain and dysfunction.

Although using the layering idea is a simplification, in the next two chapters I will describe the actual Source Connection Therapy, using the concept of the three layers described above. By viewing the therapy as a layering, I believe it will help you understand the basics. Please keep in mind that each of the touches and all of the layers representing this treatment are closely interrelated, each impacting all of the others. [Illustration 5-1]

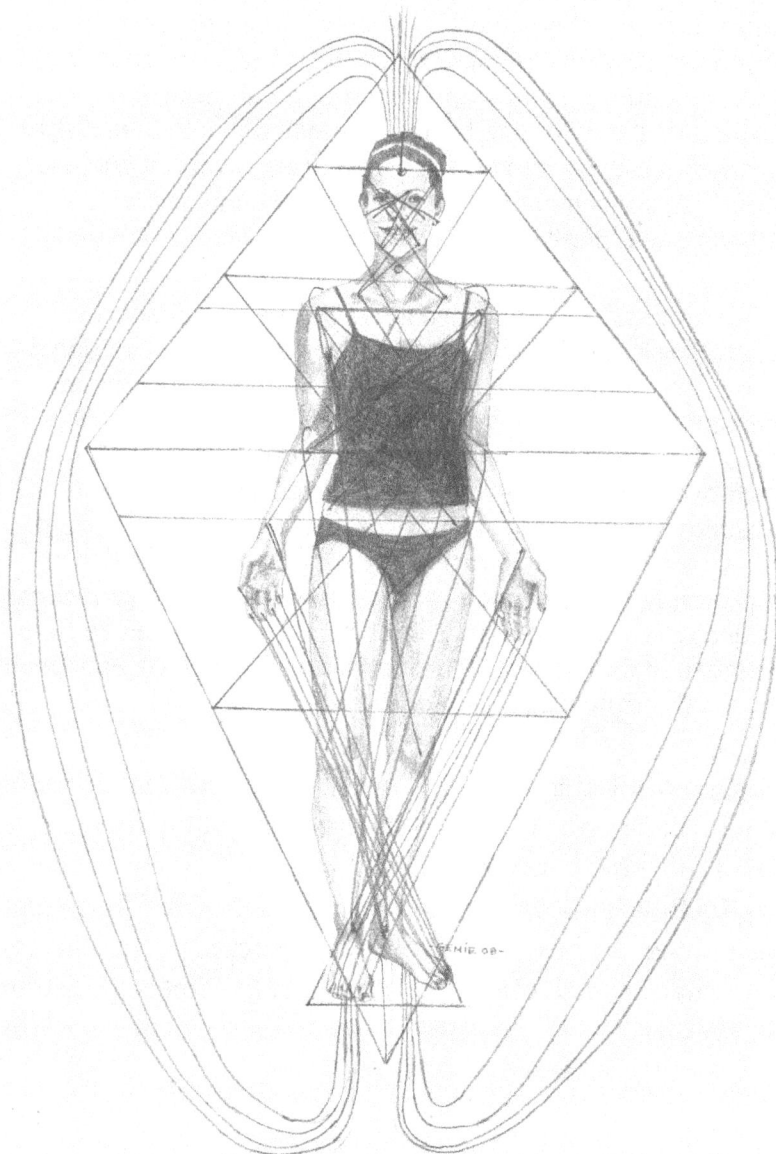

Illust. 5-1. Layers of the energetic body.

Illust. 5-2. Genie, in her father's arms.

♡

Chapter 6
Source Connection Therapy - Help Yourself

Before you can help another person by applying Source Connection Therapy, you need to be in balance yourself. In fact, to help yourself be happier and enjoy over-all better health, you should use Source Connection Therapy daily or even more often whenever you feel stressed or out of sync. Prior to describing the therapy in terms of applying it to others, I first want you to take a few minutes and work through the method of self-help. Calmly and slowly work through the examples provided in the remainder of this chapter. You'll become more balanced and begin to feel how the therapy works. You then will be better able to understand the messages another person's body will send you as you give them a Source Connection Therapy treatment.

Sometimes, it won't be possible to take the time or be in a situation where another person can help you balance. At times, because of stress at work or the daily grind, we feel uncomfortable, irritable, and out of balance. At these times, it's possible and desirable to apply the balancing techniques of Source Connection Therapy to yourself. In fact, I recommend that everyone do a self-balancing at least once a day, every day regardless of what is happening in their lives.

The body wants to be normal, upright, and balanced. Our body wants to heal itself when brought out of balance by physical, emotional, or spiritual injury. Imagine, as an example, what happens when we exercise vigorously, especially for the couch potato who is out of shape. As one exerts effort, like working out on a treadmill, body functions change rapidly, trying to adapt to the exertion. The respiratory system reacts by increasing breathing rate, maximizing the intake of oxygen. The circulatory system realizes the body has been thrown out of a steady-state balance and increases the flow of oxygen and blood to the muscles, including to the heart itself. Blood pressure increases to keep the needed volume of blood flowing. Chemicals are released into the muscles, and the nervous system accelerates its activity. The body sweats, trying to maintain a normal temperature. All of the body's systems react, trying to do the same—stay within that system's normal operating parameters. Each system protects itself.

That the body wants to maintain its normal balance is shown as soon as exertion stops. The heart and breathing slow and other systems rapidly return to their normal operating states. The body systems return to their normal levels and ideally all of the body's systems will be in balance with one another. But life isn't ideal and quite frequently, all of our various selves—physical, mental, emotional, spiritual—don't achieve the goal of balanced harmony. Unless they are all in balance, the systems won't function at their most efficient levels, which renders the person out of balance and less than healthy. For people who find themselves in difficult, critical health situations such as serious disease or injury, providing self-balancing becomes even more critical. A person confined to a hospital bed, for example, will likely feel discouraged, depressed, and helpless beyond the physical discomfort suffered from the illness or injury. One whose loved one dies, faces serious emotional and spiritual stress. Most people going through a divorce or family break up will feel frustration, confusion, and anger, all of which are made more conflicting and difficult if legal proceedings are involved. In all of these extreme situations, the person experiences a sense of unbalance, rendering him unable to heal physically, emotionally, or spiritually. For these situations, self-help Source Connection Therapy is a practical tool to help get through tough times.

More commonly, we become out of balance through our day-to-day lives. Even the demands of keeping up with work, family, and home life are enough to throw many of us off kilter. These demands often make us feel tired and less than healthy. We sometimes feel as if we can't keep up with the demands around us, feeling inadequate for the challenges we face. Trouble sleeping is common.

Whether from stress in our daily lives or from life-threatening illness, the result of being out of balance is similar—our bodies are prevented from finding the normal steady-state harmony they seek. When stress is allowed to take over our lives, illness may result, and healing is either prevented or slowed by the out of balance self. At any of these times, self-help Source Connection Therapy will be beneficial. We can be empowered to meet our obligation to be responsible for our own energy.

Because the benefits of Source Connection Therapy are cumulative, the more frequently you can do the self-balancing exercise, the better the results will be. Ideally, you should follow these self-help procedures at least daily. Whenever stress seems to be pulling you down or the world is closing in on you, taking a few minutes to relax and balance will make your day better and will certainly allow you to be more calm, assertive, and positive.

He Couldn't Sleep

A forty-eight-year-old man, on whom I had worked in person when he was visiting northern Idaho, had felt an improvement in his mental and physical wellbeing after the second treatment. Some time later, he called me from his home because he was extremely stressed at work. He was in real estate, and his business had dried up. He'd been waking at night, worrying, and not able to get back to sleep. After a lengthy period of not working at all, he felt depressed, which was made worse by not sleeping. This client hadn't made the connection between me doing the treatment when he visited me in Idaho, and the fact that he could do this treatment on himself. Feeling physical problems coming on, he called me and I led him through the balancing treatment over the phone.

We did these telephone balancing treatments at least weekly for about three months. In effect, he was doing self-treatment and I was simply acting as a guide, leading him calmly from hold to hold while he visualized them.

His sleep patterns noticeably corrected right away, especially on the nights of our phone calls. Overall improvement for this client seemed gradual to me, but to him there seemed to be a sudden awareness. During one telephone conversation, he said, "I know now what I need to do." He had been so embroiled in daily problems and so wrapped up in stress that he'd forgotten about himself as a physical, mental, and spiritual person.

I'm convinced that Source Connection Therapy opened his mind to consider what he needed. The therapy reminded him to listen to his literal body and do something about it. The treatments brought him to a realization that he needed to take care of himself, that he had a responsibility to get it together and do something good. He had reached a decision for his life, which included physical improvement, meditation classes, and he even ran a half-marathon. He has since changed careers and is now employed and doing well.

The next paragraphs describe the holds and techniques you can use by yourself to achieve balance. The rewards are many, so please enjoy these self-help Source Connection Therapy methods. Relax and smile. Allow yourself to be open, sensing the messages your body sends. Let your mind wander, opening it to the messages you may receive from Source.

Self-Help Source Connection Therapy

Being in a relaxed and comfortable environment is most helpful to gain the maximum benefit from this therapy. Do not, however, feel that you can't achieve success and an improved sense of well-being wherever you find yourself.

Below, I describe the connection holds for you to visualize. A table of the holds is provided on pages 75-76. Refer to that listing often to familiarize yourself with the holds sequence. Illustration 7-3 on page 76 and Illustration 7-4 on page 77 provide a visual reference to these holds.

You also can increase the benefits by holding these connection points with your hands. If you have mobility problems or stiffness, a few of the holds may be a little difficult to physically touch. In that case, just touch those that you can and use the visualizations described below for the remaining connection points. Physically touching the connections points can be done with either hand, yet crossing the body using the right hand to make touches on the left side and vice versa have a physical benefit, especially for people who, because of age or infirmity, have movement limitations. You can use your fingers or palms of either hand, but all of your connection touches should be gentle and used in conjunction with clear visualizations. Take your time and move slowly, calmly, and with purpose. [Illustration 6-1]

Begin your therapy by taking a long, slow, deep breath, hold it a short time, then slowly exhale, relaxing your muscles as you do so.

While focusing your thoughts, become aware of your right shoulder. Visualize a connection between your right shoulder and your left hip. Mentally picture this connection as a very bright white or golden light crossing the mid-line of your body. Have a clear picture in your mind of how this looks, and feel the connection. Calmly, mentally move this connection and visualize this same connection between your right shoulder and your left knee. See and feel this connection.

Now, staying focused on the right shoulder, take a deep breath, exhale, and visualize a connection between your right shoulder and your left

Illust. 6-1. Self-treatment holds example.

inside ankle bone. This is a long electrical current that urges a connection between the upper half of your body to the lower half. This works with your motor function and helps with physical balance.

> In myofascial release classes, I've seen people who are not energetically connected between their upper and lower halves. They exhibit a number of physical problems such as motor function problems, lack of balance, possible vertigo. Some couldn't even stand on one foot without tipping over. Sometimes, we see people who fit the description of *having their head in the clouds and their feet not touching the ground.* These people are experiencing disruptions of the long electrical connections, which can be caused by a number of issues. Quite often, these are the result of serious accidents that left them disconnected in complex ways. At this point, when evaluating and talking with a client, you may become aware that the client needs other professionals for specialized help. In cases like this, working as a team with other medical professionals is most effective.

Inhale and slowly exhale as you move to the next connection points. Change your holds and feel the connection between your left inside ankle bone and your right elbow. During this hold you may feel an electrical spark or a warm feeling between the connection points. This should not feel uncomfortable, but you may feel a slowing, relaxing, and calming of the central nervous system and the lowering of blood pressure.

Visualize the next connection, between your left inside ankle bone and your right wrist. See this connection and feel it, experiencing similar feelings to the previous holds.

You now should feel relaxed and sense a shift in your consciousness. Experience how good you are feeling as your body is becoming more integrated. What you are feeling is your body's way of reuniting those connection points that had been broken and lost previously. These connection points are coming together, helping your body, emotions, and spirit become balanced.

Visualize the connection between your left great toe and your right thumb. Hold that image for up to a minute, then see in sequence the connection points between each one of your fingers on your right hand to the corresponding toe on your left foot, moving from great toe and thumb to small toe and little finger. These points are connecting your extremities, and you should feel an energetic sensation as your body's connections are being made. These connections are firming and energizing connections. They will allow you to be energized, yet relaxed. Being energized does not mean fragmented; rather, your body will feel neither lethargic nor hyper. You will feel calm, but with purpose and focus.

Now, shift your total focus to the other side of your body where you will visualize and renew connections in the same order as described above. Each set of holds, again, passes through and across the mid-line of your body. Take a deep breath in and slowly exhale. Relax.

As you repeat the visualized holds, you form the important energy grids that strengthen your core. Check the integrity of these visualized holds and calmly take in the feeling of your body making these connections. As you visualize the holds on this side of your body, you will feel a sense of calming, of deeper relaxation.

After you've completed visualizations of the connection points from both sides of your body, shift your focus to the mid-section of your body. Take a breath and, as you exhale, visualize and feel the connection between your right rib, about two inches below your sternum, and your left clavicle (collar bone). This connection opens the Heart Chakra. As the Chakra opens, it connects your body to your spirit while keeping you protected from incoming negative energies, your personal fears and outside stressors. [See Illustration 6-2, page 67]

The Rib to Clavicle Connection

Often when we are injured, either physically or emotionally (when we are hurt), we feel wounded. Frequently we respond by closing our heart (feeling like your heart is broken) which closes our Heart Chakra. This closing of the heart results in poor communication with others and spirit. Depression and physical restrictions result quite often. Unfortunately, people are treated with anti-depressants or turn to self-medication, alcohol, and other destructive methods of coping. These methods of treatment don't solve the underlying problems because they tend to mask the hurt, sometimes leading to more serious physical and mental problems.

As you practice keeping your Heart Chakra open, you

will feel lighter, more joyous, and an internal willingness to find solutions. If you mask pain or sadness, you deny your body's natural ability to correct and balance itself. Emotional or physical pain is your body's way of telling you that something needs to change. Physical pain indicates a need to resolve an issue with your body. If you cut your finger, the pain and the blood tell you that you need to fix it. Pain and pressure in your chest may be a heart attack, not something requiring heartburn medication.

Emotional pain—feeling the loss of a loved one or romantic break up, for example—is exactly the same. This emotional pain is telling you to follow the natural course and grieve and move on. Crying or otherwise letting the pain out is normal. It is your natural way of healing emotional pain. Because we have become so immersed in working and rushing, we tend to seek instant solutions.

There's a pill for that, seems to be our society's way of dealing with emotional pain. Our society encourages us to turn to masking agents rather than fixing the underlying problems. I encourage you to look deep and find the root cause of an emotional problem, then deal with it directly and naturally to the fullest extent you can. If your pain is severe, seek professional help, but please be cautious about prescriptions that are offered too quickly.

Maintaining a calm demeanor, shift your focus to form a connection between your left rib and your right collar bone. Visualize this connection, feel it and breathe it. As with other connections, see this as a bright white or golden light crossing through your body. Visualize this light as forming a bridge, a connection between the hold points.

Moving your attention toward a connection between your body and your head, visualize a connection between your left collar bone and the right side of your chin. You are connecting your words with your feelings, enhancing your ability to communicate.

Hold this image. Breathe. Exhale and move your visualization to a connection between your right collar bone and the left side of your chin. See and feel this connection. Notice how your body becomes even more relaxed as these connections are made and held.

On your next breath, see the connection from your right collar bone to the left side of your head, approximately two inches above your left ear. After holding this picture, calmly move these connections points with your mind so you form a connection between your left collar bone and the right side of the top of your head about two inches above your right ear.

When you make connections between the head and collar bone, you likely will experience a deep sense of calm; breathing patterns will become more quiet. The cranial system is reorganizing. All touching of the facial bones needs to be very gentle.

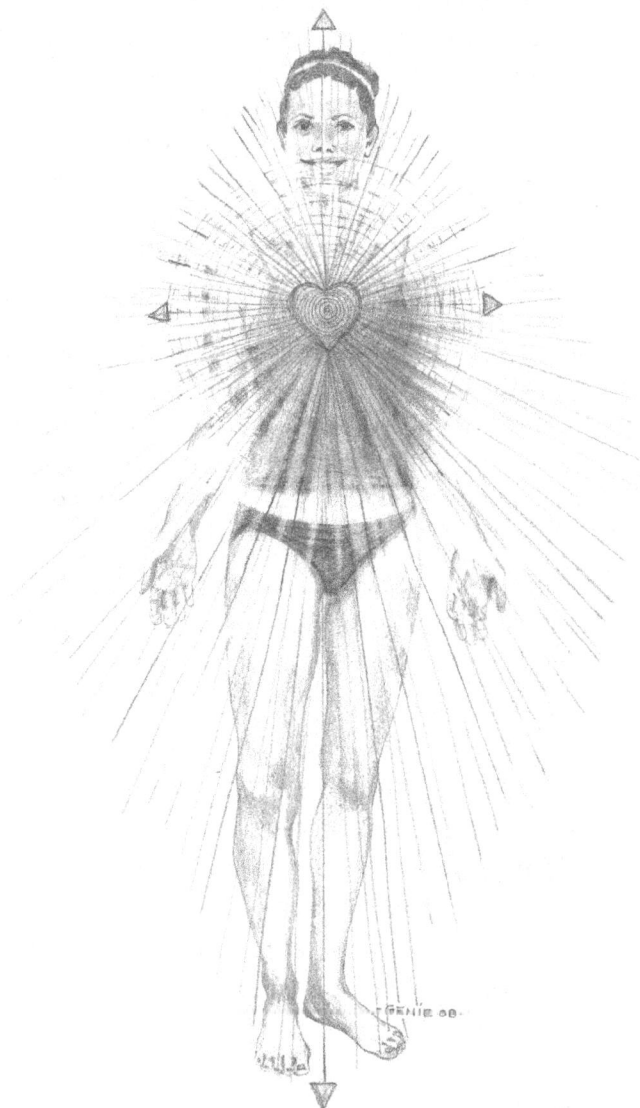

Illust. 6-2. Heart Chakra, when open.

Breathe and visualize the next connection, forming a line between the right side of the top of your head to the left side of your chin. Now, make this connection between the left side of the top of your head and the right side of your chin. This set of holds balances how you take in external information and then process it. All the while the cranial system continues to balance.

Enjoy the feeling as you become more balanced with each connection point. Take your time, enjoy the calming, relaxing feelings.

Visualize the connection between the right side of your chin to the left eyebrow area, close to your nose. After focusing for a minute or so on that hold, change your picture to imagine a connection between the left side of your chin and the right eyebrow area close to your nose. See and feel these connections, breathing it all in. Connections to both audio and visual are made with these holds. Through this process you will continue opening yourself to Source, becoming more able to access and receive information.

See and feel the connection from your right eyebrow to your left cheek. Breathe and feel this connection, then move your focus to imagine the connection between your left eyebrow and your right cheek. This set of connection holds works with your cheek bones, facial bones, and provides further craniosacral system relief. You may notice an opening of sinuses and pressure release in sinus areas.

Continue making these connections, breathing and feeling the changes your body is making.

Now, visualize a connection between your right eyebrow and your left earlobe. Breathe in this hold, then change and make a mental connection between your left eyebrow and your right earlobe. Know that when these connections are made, they reunite your thoughts with your intuition. Breathe slowly and deeply and visualize these connections. This hold also is audio and visual. It will open your ability to hear and see even though you may not feel anything specific because you are deeply relaxed and your body is spending its time reorganizing and connecting.

Your final visualized connection is from your Third Eye Chakra, the center of your forehead, to the top of your head. Maintain this connection, seeing and feeling it, sensing your physical, emotional, and spiritual selves joining and balancing with one another. By this time your body's electro-magnetic fields are clear, your body is quiet, calm, and receptive to your Source's information on what you need to be healthy and strong.

Third eye intuition opens you to hearing what you need from Source. You are getting cues from your Source about what you should be doing, how to lead the best life you can. You are open to receive information on how to live your life through any adversity, how to cope with daily setbacks. Sometimes you will just get information on how to heal from an injury or how to take the next step for your personal growth. Staying in balance with your Source is the way to find happiness because you'll be open to Source and will hear the correct information for your life. [See Illustration 6-3, page 70]

Remain calm and relaxed for a few minutes if demands on your time allow.

Consider doing these balancing, calming exercises every morning and evening and please don't hesitate to apply them any time you're feeling disconnected or fragmented.

After each Source Connection Therapy session, you will be brought into the moment. You will feel the sensation and improved self-esteem that living in the moment can bring. It brings you joy, not discouragement and frustration you often find if living in the past. Source Connection Therapy helps you fulfill the personal obligation of a 24/7 commitment to self. Feel the connection and feel the difference.

Once you begin treatment on others, as described in the next chapter, don't stop your own self-help Source Connection Therapy because it will cause fragmentation, pulling at your emotions and spirit rather than making all of the connections. Fragmenting in any aspect of your life results in imbalance. If time is limited or you are interrupted by work or other demands, shorten the time for each visualized hold and complete the whole series if you can. If you can't complete the full protocol, consider finding time later in that day and try again to balance by completing the full therapy session.

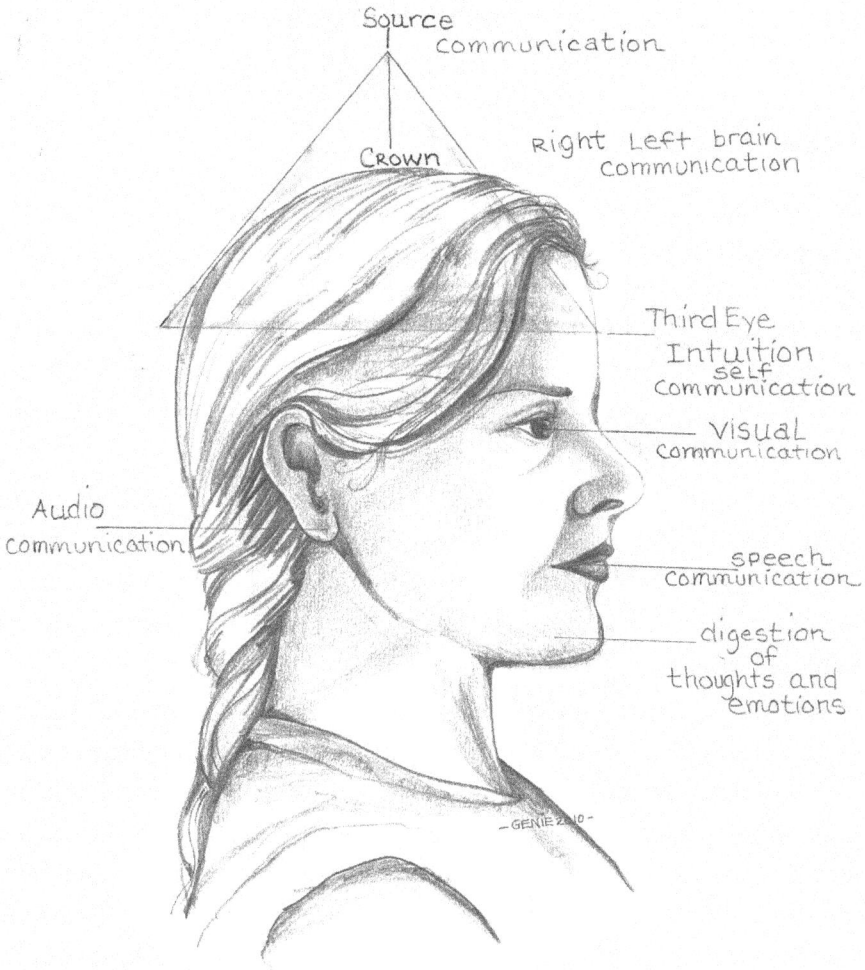

Source
communication

Crown

Right Left brain
communication

Third Eye
Intuition
self
communication

Visual
communication

Audio
communication

speech
communication

digestion
of
thoughts and
emotions

—GENIE 2010—

Illust. 6-3. Diagram of head and connection to Source.

Chapter 7
Source Connection Therapy, Applying the Treatment on Others

The Treatment in General

*F*or a therapist applying Source Connection Therapy to a client or for a lay-person using this protocol to help another person, the techniques and application of holds are the same. Unlike massage therapy and many of the *touch therapies*, the holds used in Source Connection Therapy aren't intended to manipulate or change any skeletal or muscular structures. Rather, all holds are to be applied gently. In all of the holds used on the body, one can use finger tips or the palm of the hands.

For holds on the face and head, the holds need to be especially gentle, using the fingertips because the facial bones are affected and the spaces are so very small. In craniosacral treatments, for example, the touches are similar to those used here, affecting craniosacral rhythms and the energetic patterns they are linking.

If your intentions are to use this therapy as a treatment protocol in your professional practice, I recommend you take a class in Source Connection Therapy. This continuing education class includes lecture, discussion, and hands-on practical application. These classes cover about sixteen hours of instructions and application. It will boost your confidence and expand your credentials. You'll gain the most benefit and knowledge by studying beyond the contents of this book. I also offer teacher certification courses.

Ideally, the therapy should be used in a calming environment. It begins with the person receiving the treatment (whom I will refer to as the client) lying in supine position (on her back). For a person unable to get onto a massage table—or if you don't have a table—the client may lie on the floor, a bed, or a sofa if it allows the person applying the holds to move all the way around the client. In some cases, it may be necessary or desirable to have the client sitting in a chair or wheel chair. [Illustration 7-1].

Illust. 7-1. Using chair or wheelchair for therapy.

Often, if you're working on a family member or person to whom you are emotionally close, you should take extra care to be certain you're relaxed, and remain so, and not be attached to the outcome. Your energetic expectations can spill over onto another person's energy, which can impede the treatment. The premise of Source Connection Therapy is for each to be self-contained and not to impose our will on the other. Our energetic communication needs to be with Source, not with the therapist or client.

It's important in every case for the person applying this treatment to another to balance herself before she begins. The therapist should follow the examples in the previous chapter on how to apply Source Connection Therapy to herself. Anyone applying this therapy or other touch therapies must recognize that whenever we touch another person, energy is shared. This transfer of energy is shared in both directions—from the client to the technician and from the technician back to the client—thus, we each need to be responsible for our own energies. We also need to be responsible to others whom we touch. To disregard this responsibility may bring the person out of balance, achieving the exact opposite result from that which we intend.

The person applying the holds (the therapist) begins by standing or kneeling in a comfortable position at the side of the client. You can start with either side of the client, but you'll complete all holds on both sides of the client's body. Both people should be comfortable and the surroundings as relaxing as possible.

I realize that for most people this will require some adaptation and imagination. Not everyone, after all, has a massage therapy table at home. There is no time limit on the holds, but holding each for a minute or longer will give the body time to firm up that connection.

With practice, a person applying this treatment will recognize the correct amount of time because the energetic holds will feel dynamic and solid. Some people have told me they can see the connections changing from weak and fragmented to dynamic and firm. During the full time of the treatment, it's important not to disconnect from the person. Always have at least one hand touching the person receiving the therapy. Disconnecting disrupts the therapeutic balancing effects.

As you apply the Source Connection Therapy holds, you'll note they cross the body's mid-line from left to right and right to left. This also reunites the masculine (generally considered to be the right side) with the feminine (left side). Feminine is generally associated with intuition, gentle strength, while masculine is thought of as power and moving forward. When these two energies are balanced, we are more able to intuitively and calmly move forward toward our highest good.

As shown in Illustration 7-2, boney landmarks serve as a guide for placing some of the holds described below. [Illustration 7-2]

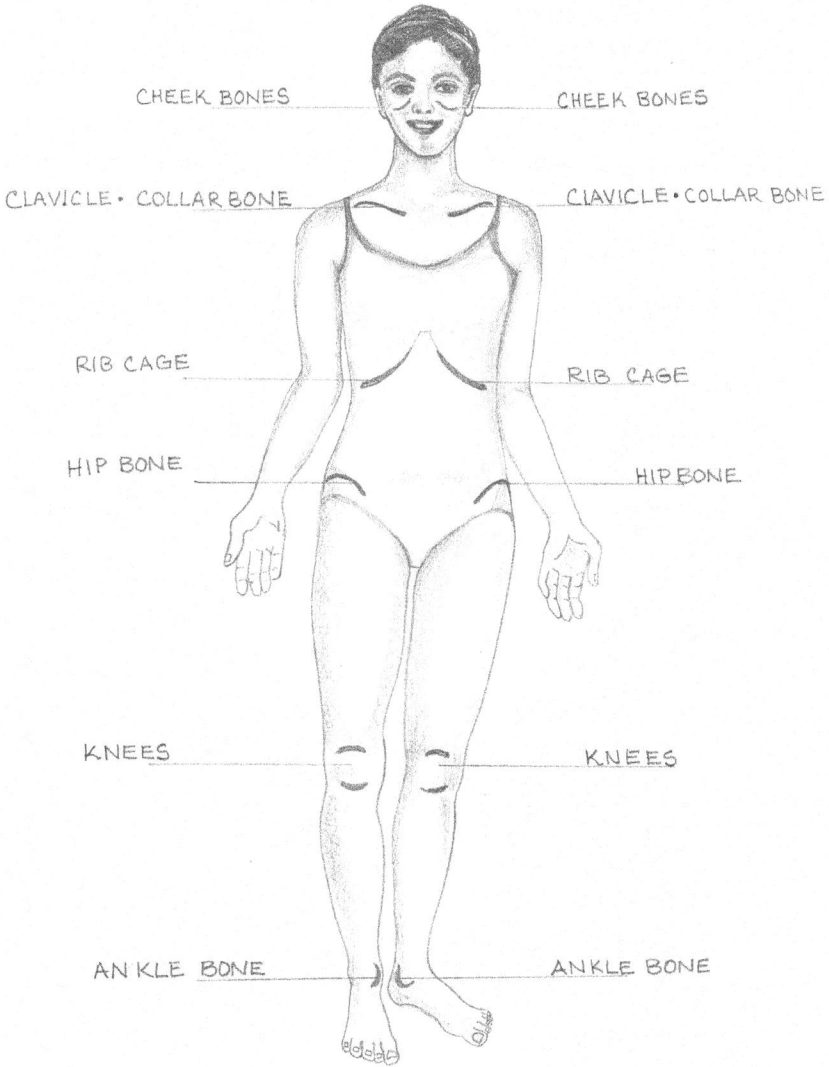

CHEEK BONES   CHEEK BONES

CLAVICLE • COLLAR BONE   CLAVICLE • COLLAR BONE

RIB CAGE   RIB CAGE

HIP BONE   HIP BONE

KNEES   KNEES

ANKLE BONE   ANKLE BONE

Illust. 7-2. Boney landmarks. Guide to position of certain holds.

Layer One - Opening and Clearing
the Electro-Magnetic Fields (human aura)

The first set of holds, which I described above as Layer One, opens and clears the client's physical systems, so they accept the reminders the holds will provide. This layer of holds also works the electro-magnetic fields, firming the fields to provide protection from outside sources during the remainder of the protocol.

I've provided an Illustration for each of the holds, along with text to aid in your understanding of how to do the connection holds. The descriptions and illustration only cover the holds on one side of the body. You will apply them on both sides to complete the full treatment.

To help you keep this straight, I've listed the sequence of holds below:

Hold Sequence Table

Start on either side of body

1. scapula and opposing hip bone
2. anterior shoulder to opposing knee
3. anterior shoulder to ankle bone
4. elbow to ankle bone
5. wrist to ankle bone
6. thumb to opposing great toe

7 - 10. each finger to each opposing toe

11 -20. Without disconnecting from the client, repeat the above sequence on the other side of the body.

21. clavicle to opposing side rib cage

22. repeat hold on opposite sides

23. clavicle to opposite jaw

24. repeat hold on opposite sides

25. clavicle to opposite side of head

26. repeat hold on opposite sides

27. side of head to opposing jaw

28. repeat hold on opposite sides

29. jaw to opposing brow

30. repeat hold on opposite sides

31. brow to opposing cheek

32. repeat hold on opposite sides

33. brow to opposing earlobe, pulling earlobe down slightly

34. repeat hold on opposite sides

35. middle of forehead to top of head

When all holds are complete, slowly remove hands from client and allow some quiet time

Please remember to complete all holds on both sides of the client's body. A total of twenty holds comprise this first layer of connections, which firm up the electro-magnetic fields. The following descriptions and illustrations are for the first ten only, but should provide guidance in completing all twenty. [Illustration 7-3 and Illustration 7-4]

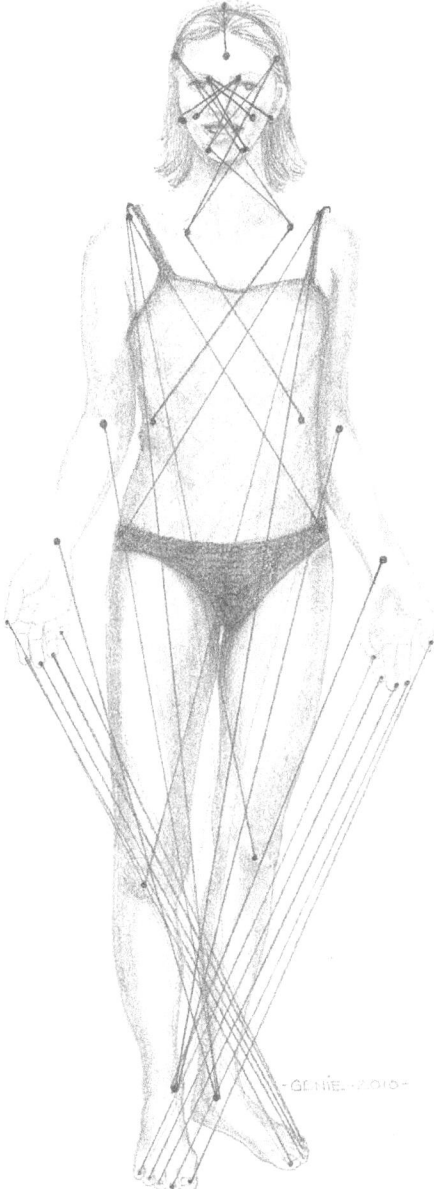

Illust. 7-3. Shows connection lines for clarity.

Illust. 7-4. Face hold placement, numbered for clarity.

Scapula to Opposite Hip

The therapist gently reaches under the client's shoulder and places her hand on the client's shoulder blade. She places her other hand on the client's opposite hip, forming a connection which crosses the body's midline. [Illustration 7-5]

Illust. 7-5. Scapula to opposite hip.

This hold raises the vibration of the internal structure from one large flat bone to another large flat bone, increasing the integrity of those bones. This positively influences all the tissue and organs between these points. After the connection firms, the electro-magnetic fields along this line are realigned, reorganized. This also reminds the right and left brain hemispheres to work together.

Shoulder Front to Opposite Knee

The therapist, while always keeping contact with the client, slides her hand from the scapula to the front of the shoulder. The other hand moves from the hip to the knee forming another connection across the mid-line of the body. [Illustration 7-6]

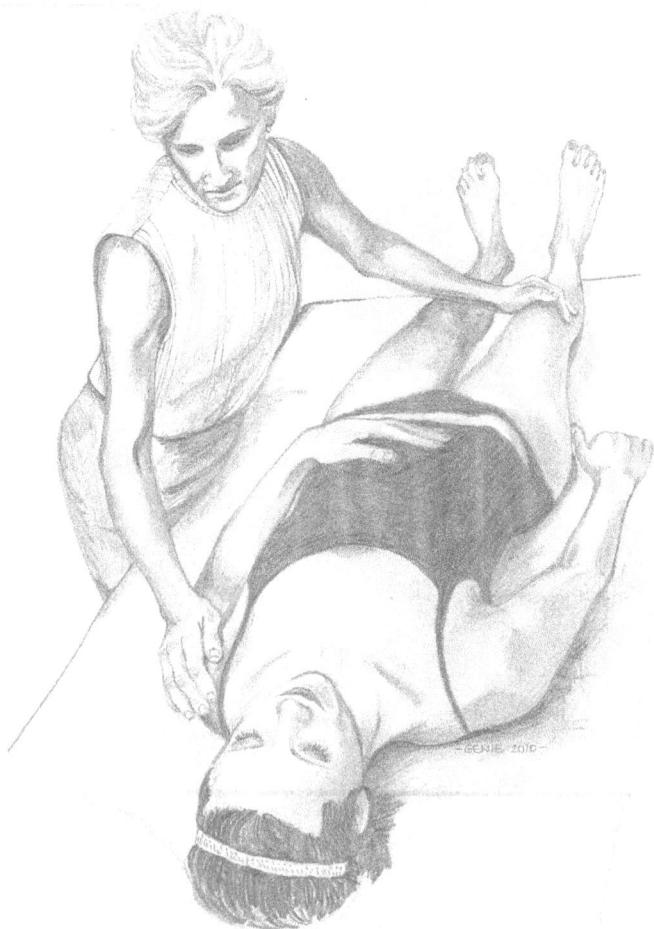

Illust. 7-6. Anterior shoulder to opposite knee.

As this series of holds progresses, they further energize the right and left brain, while engaging the central nervous system and alerting the motor nerves, which are about movement. You also are opening the peripheral Chakras, which are located at all of the joints. These peripheral Chakras are secondary places on the body, which take in energy from outside. The energy you receive through your hand, for example, goes to your Heart Chakra via the peripherals.

The therapist may feel or notice changes in the physical body of the client. The client may be more relaxed, breathing slower, and often becoming more quiet. If the client has been in pain, that pain may be subsiding; if nervous or agitated, the client may become more calm.

Shoulder to Inside Ankle Bone

One hand remains on the shoulder, while the other hand is moved from the knee to the ankle bone. The person applying the holds will gently touch the inside of the ankle bone, the bump on the inside of the ankle. [Illustration 7-7] You may need to ask the person receiving the treatment to bend her leg because this, for many people, is a long reach. This is the location of another peripheral Chakra. NOTE: See Illustration 7-2 for boney landmarks.

This hold further clears the electro-magnetic field as it also opens the Chakras. This hold connects a long energetic current, allowing the client to feel aware, but not hyper. It increases the protection of the electro-magnetic field from negative outside forces. This therapy feels so good because we create a safety zone within which the body, mind, and spirit can regroup and reorganize. This hold begins building that safety zone. The therapist may feel a slight vibration or electrical charge. Sometimes, the client will even ask questions about what they are feeling.

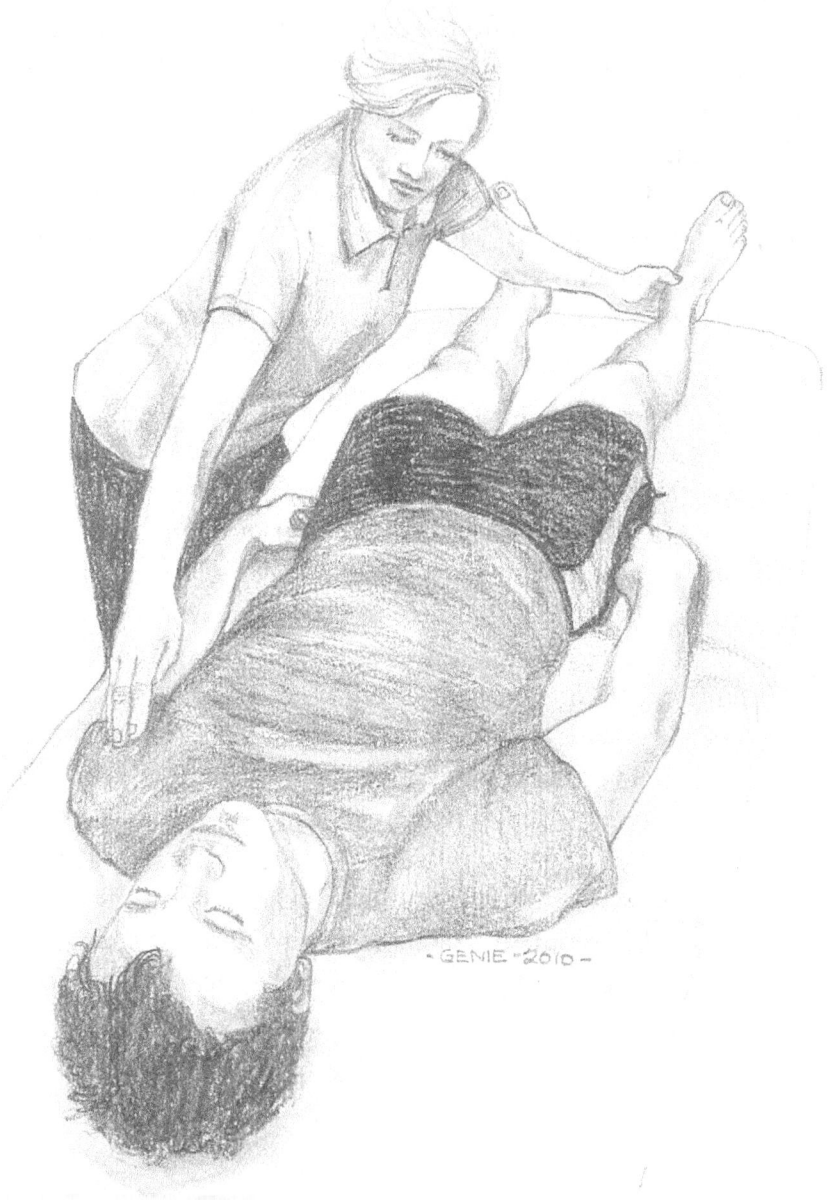

Illust. 7-7. Shoulder to inside ankle bone opposite leg.

Elbow to Inside Ankle Bone

The hand on the ankle bone remains where it is, while the other hand moves down to the client's elbow. [Illustration 7-8]

This connection, like all of the connections in this layer of treatment, is further aligning and opening the electro-magnetic fields. The elbow is another peripheral Chakra. Again, right and left brain are reunited. The masculine/feminine are becoming more balanced and the electro-magnetic fields continue aligning.

The client should feel deep relaxation with an increasing awareness of her subconscious. An enhanced awareness of Source often begins during this phase of the treatment and becomes stronger as progressive holds are completed.

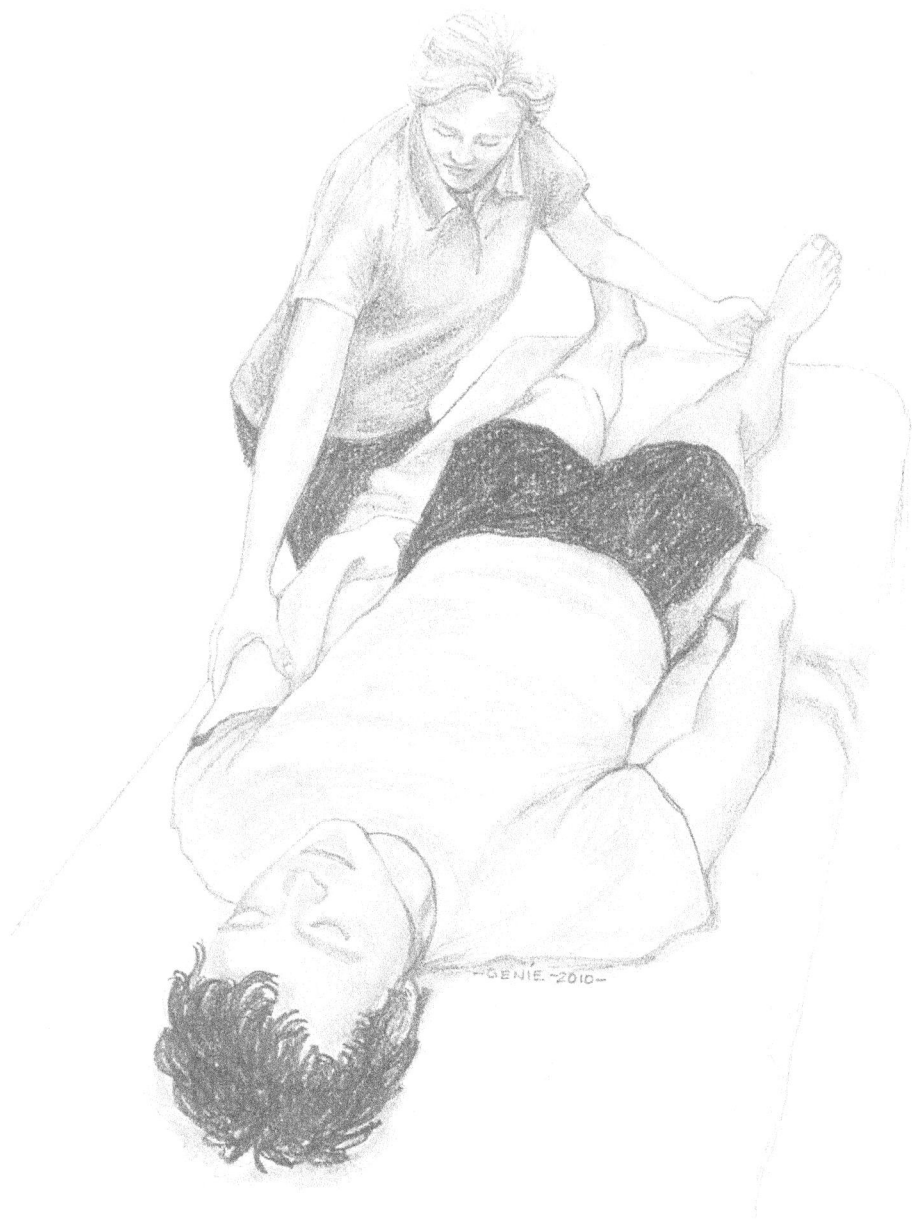

Illust. 7-8. Elbow to inside ankle bone opposite leg.

Wrist to Opposite Inside Ankle Bone

The hand remains on the ankle as the other hand moves down the arm to the wrist, another peripheral Chakra. This wrist to ankle bone connection hold is very effective in opening the electro-magnetic fields because its connection is from points near the extremities. This hold is a significant step in building your safety zone. [Illustration 7-9]

The client may feel an energy boost during this hold. The therapist should keep in mind that these initial holds may take a long time to connect, depending on how balanced the client's whole body was at the beginning of the treatment.

Illust. 7-9. Wrist to opposite ankle bone.

Finger and Toes

This set of holds connects your body's extremities, establishing protective fields. They are about balance (feet) and communication (hands). They help keep you firmly connected to Source and all other beings.

Beginning with the thumb and the great toe on the opposite side of the client's body, the therapist holds the client's thumb between her thumb and forefinger with one hand and the opposite great toe between thumb and forefinger of the other hand. [Illustration 7-10]

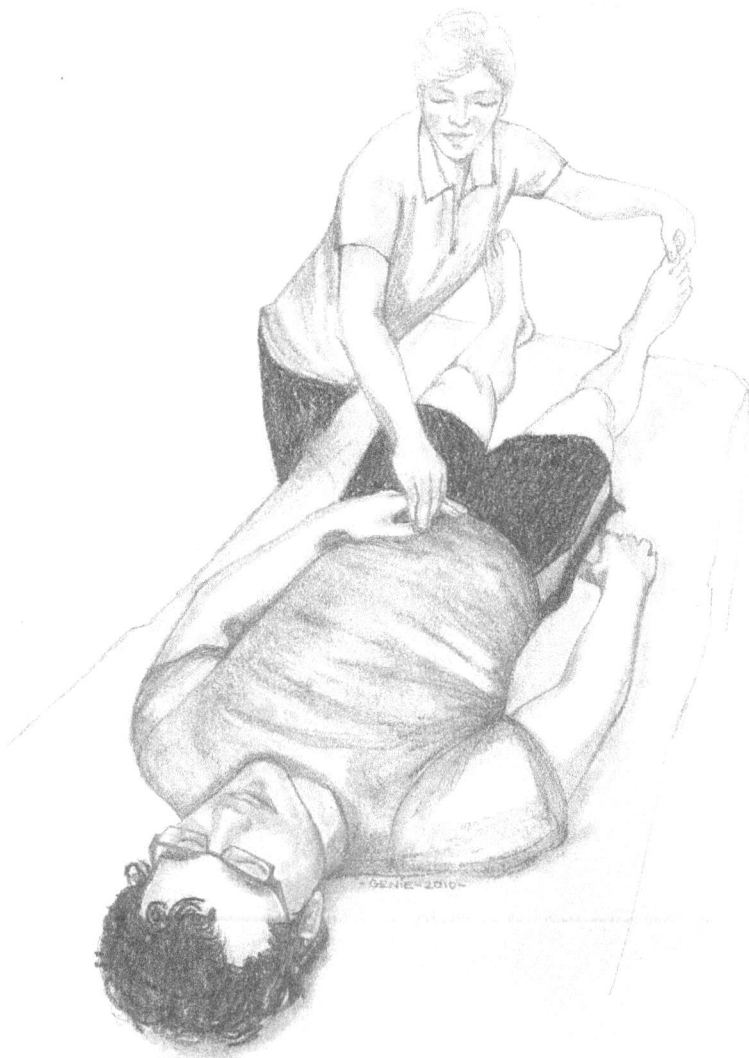

Illust. 7-10. Thumb to opposite great toe.

Allowing sufficient time with each hold, the therapist then moves along the digits, making connections between the forefinger (index finger) and second toe [Illustration 7-11]

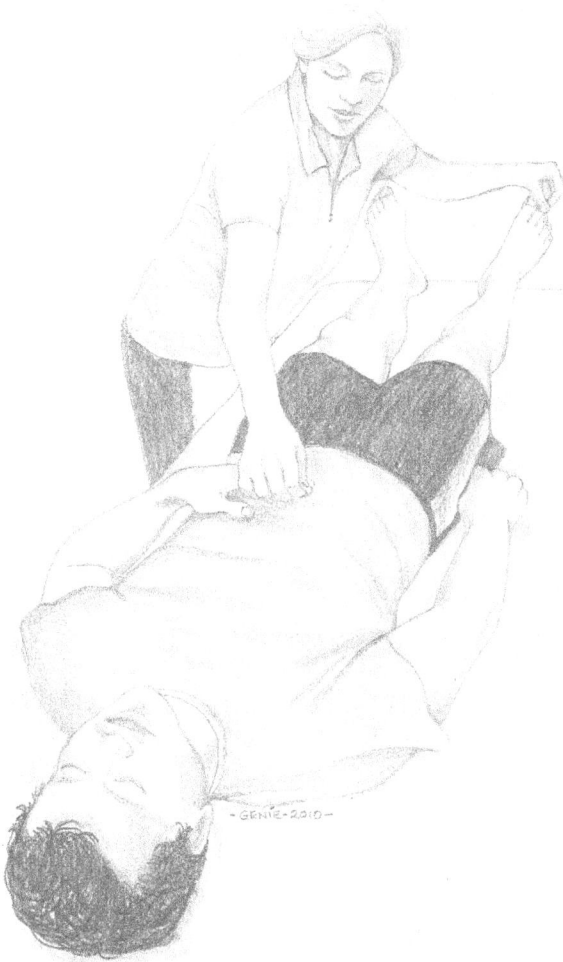

Illust. 7-11. Forefinger to opposite second toe.

...the middle finger and middle toe [Illustration 7-12]...

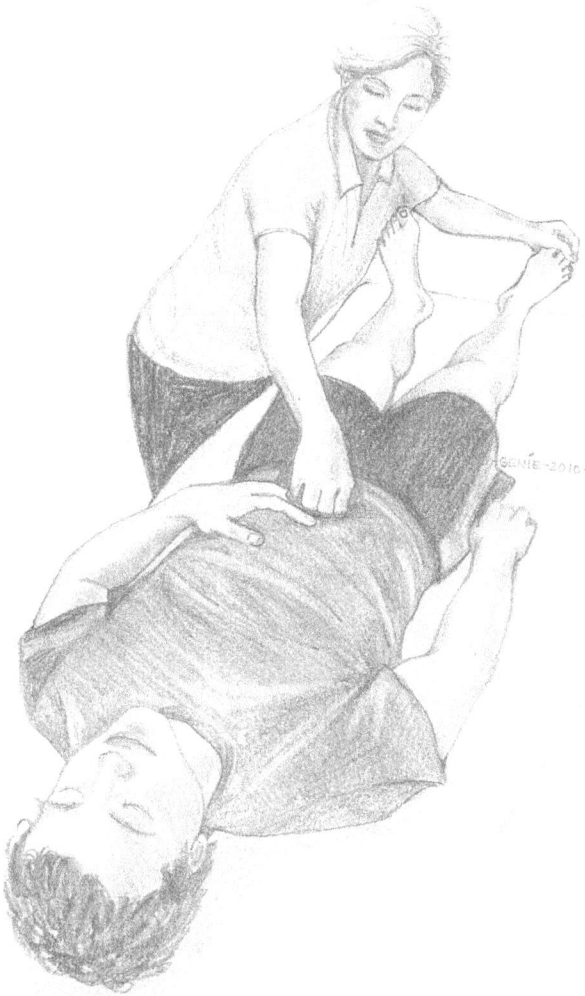

Illust. 7-12. Middle finger to opposite middle toe.

...the ring finger and the fourth toe [Illustration 7-13]...

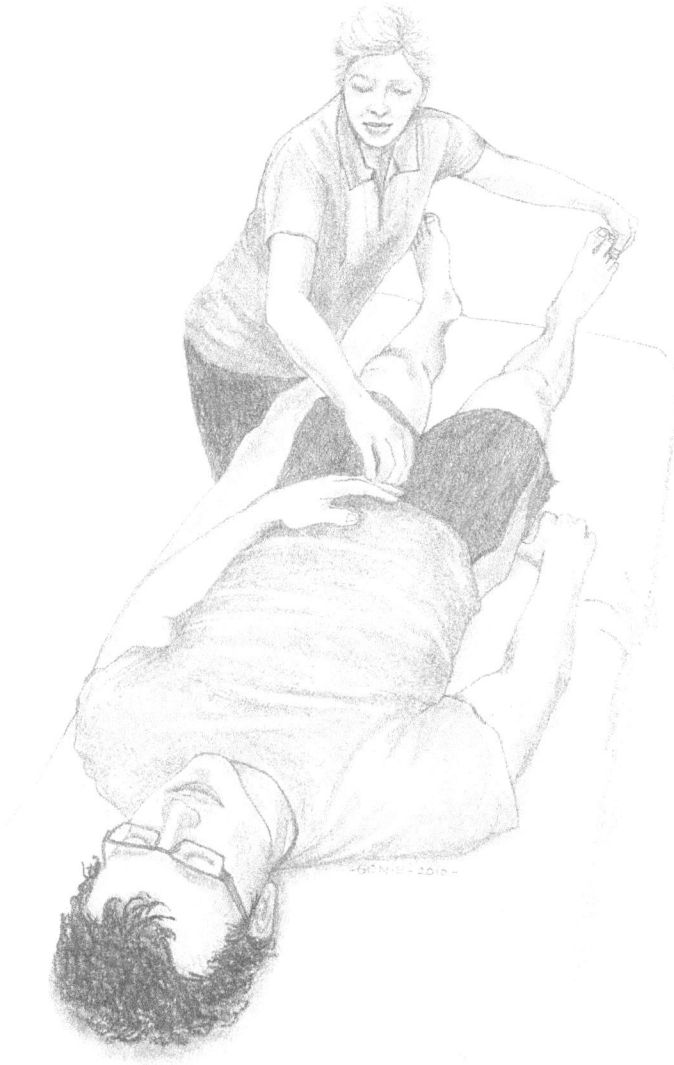

Illust. 7-13. Ring finger to opposite fourth toe.

...the pinky finger and small toe [Illustration 7-14] without disconnecting (always keeping one hand in contact with the client).

Illust. 7-14. Pinky finger to opposite small toe.

Without disconnecting from the client's body, move to the other side of the body. Starting with the scapula, repeat in a calm, gentle manner all the holds described above. When doing the same holds on the opposite side of the client's body, these holds may not take as long because the body has already started the reorganization process.

As you work through these connection holds on the opposite side, the Cross Pattern Connections form a grid. This firms the body's energies and strengthens the core. In addition to all the beneficial effects and impacts on the Chakras and electro-magnetic fields, this grid engages the body's safety zone. Similar to constructing a building, the cross pattern grids form a solid structure with a strong core.

In addition to strengthening the core, the holds on the opposite side of the body get the figure-eight flow patterns moving, setting the body in a safe, receptive place for healing. [Eden, 201-03]. This figure-eight flow pattern, resulting from the cross-body connections, enhances connection of the left and right brain hemispheres. [Eden, 203]. The crossover patterns at this phase of the treatment put the body into a receptive mode.

Layer Two – Further Shoring Up the Core

Clavicle to Rib

Without disconnecting, move up the side of the client's body, touching the clavicle on one side and the rib on the opposite side. [Illustrations 7-15]

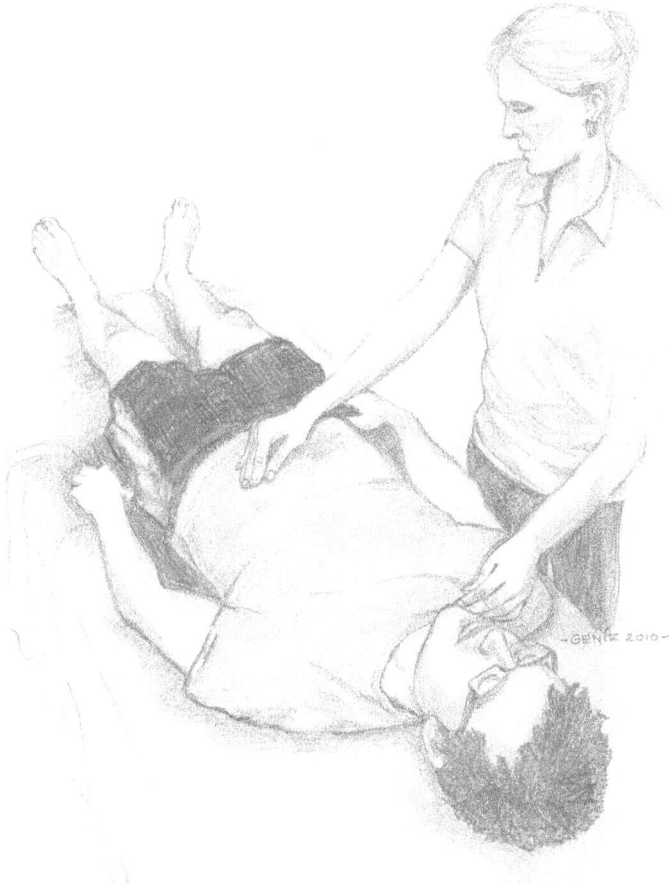

Illust. 7-15. Right clavicle to left rib.

...and [Illustration 7-16].

Illust. 7-16. Left clavicle to right rib.

As shown previously in Illustration 7-2, the proper location of the rib hold is about three fingers down from the client's sternum. It's the solid bone connecting ribs in the center of the chest. This hold affects your core—heart and spleen function, digestion, circulation, and respiration. This hold continues the firming of the energetic cross patterns of the body, while further opening the Heart Chakra.

Without disconnecting from the clavicle hold point, move the hand from the rib and place it on the opposite side clavicle. Then move the other hand from the clavicle to the rib on the remaining side. These two holds form a large **X** as the clavicles are connected with the ribs on opposite sides. [Illustration 7-17].

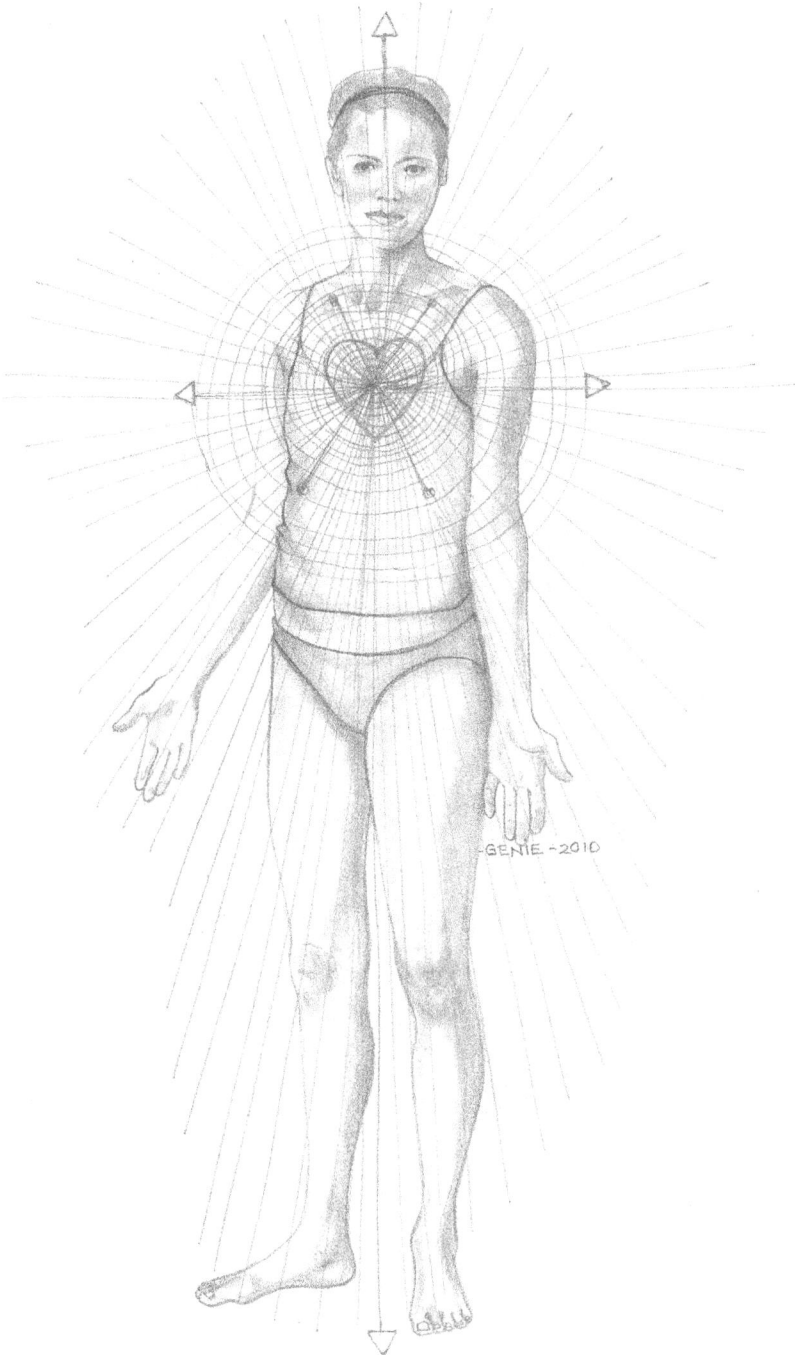

Illust. 7-17. Heart X pattern.

Generally, at this point in the therapy, it's common to see the body go into deep relaxation and reorganization. I almost always see this relaxation happen at this phase of the treatment, which manifests in eyelids fluttering, a deep breath or sigh. The client may experience a feeling of the body sinking. The blood pressure is lowering and the central nervous system is calm, enabling the body to be in a deep state of reorganization and healing.

Still Point

As the client relaxes, his or her body and mind are given a quiet moment for deep relaxation and reorganization, which we refer to as a still point. A still point can be spontaneous or induced through therapy. In its simplest terms, the still point is a time during which cranial wave formations subside or cease. Most often, the client will feel euphoric for the short time the still point lasts.

A still point during Source Connection Therapy or craniosacral therapy is significant because it's during this time that old, dysfunctional cranial wave patterns are discarded. As new, more positive cranial wave patterns emerge, the still point ends.

During Source Connection Therapy, I think of the still point as a quiet reorganization of the functioning body. This explains why we can change old habits and substitute new, positive habits. This is the time when the magic happens.

Forming the **X** across the chest opens the Heart Chakra, making a connection between the spiritual and the physical—connecting head to heart. From a physiological view, this layer of treatment is identifiable as balancing and stimulating production and re-absorption of cerebral spinal fluid.

From the spiritual view, as the heart and head are connected, the heart Chakra opens and you become stronger. With the heart Chakra open, you will be able to protect and keep your boundaries firm. If the heart Chakra is closed, it forms a barrier to the outside world and you become walled-off and enclosed. With an open Heart Chakra, however, a powerful energy field protects you, yet allows you to take in energy.

Forming energetic protection by opening the heart Chakra makes available the strength needed to connect to Source, self, and the ability to firm up your boundaries. This firming allows energies to work properly. This layer of treatment bridges the gap between physical and spiritual, which requires your body to feel safe. With the first set of holds, we set the stage, clearing the debris and opening the body to feel safe (safety zone). The holds forming the **X** across the chest are the bridge between physical and spiritual.

Layer Three – Connecting Head to Body

The holds in this layer of treatment bring together intuition and logic, heart and brain, emotion and thought. This layer connects speech with your emotions and actions, allowing you to communicate your needs and desires in a positive, assertive manner.

For guidance in making the holds in this layer of treatment, take a moment to study Illustration 7-18 below, which shows an overview of all the cranial connections. You'll see the grid pattern forming up the front of the face, with specific hand placement points for the therapist's touches. [Illustration 7-18].

Illust. 7-18. Overview of cranial connections.

The cranialsacral system comes into balance in this layer of the protocols with the facial bone holds. The head to body connection opens the Throat Chakra, and also reunites your speech with your hearing. The Throat Chakra, the Third Eye Chakra (the Sixth Chakra, and the Crown Chakra (Seventh Chakra) are all being balanced, bringing you into alignment with your Source. These holds help you become self-contained, and it opens a direct-line connection to your Source.

Clavicle to Jaw

Without losing contact with the client, the therapist will stand at the client's head as seen in Illustrations 7-19 and 7-20. As the therapist concludes the above clavicle to rib holds, he should move the hand from the rib to the clavicle so one hand is placed on each clavicle (match hands on the clavicles. From this position, the therapist moves one hand from a clavicle to the opposite jaw, gently placing finger tips about two finger widths from the center of the chin. [Illustration 7-19]

Illust. 7-19. Right clavicle to left jaw.

If the therapist started with the right clavicle and left jaw, the jaw hold should be to the left of center on the jaw. [Illustration 7-20]. When the therapist feels it is time to move to the opposite side, match hands on the clavicles again, then move one hand to the opposite side jaw, simply reversing the holds.

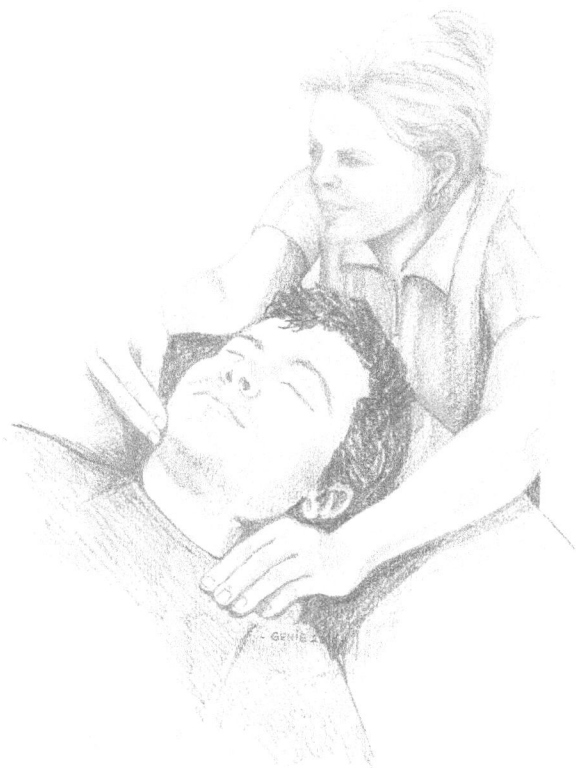

Illust. 7-20. Left clavicle to right jaw.

The clavicle to jaw holds are the next step in the continuum of the physical body's connection with the mental and spiritual body. You're reminding the brain that it has a body upon which it depends to get around and to survive. As the cross connections are made, both right and left brain hemispheres are reminded to work together cooperatively and to be in strong contact with the body.

Clavicle to Side of Head

Following the previous hold, the therapist should once again match hands on the clavicles, moving the one hand from the jaw to the clavicle. Then the therapist moves one hand from the clavicle to the opposite side of the head and the other hand remains on the clavicle. [Illustration 7-21]

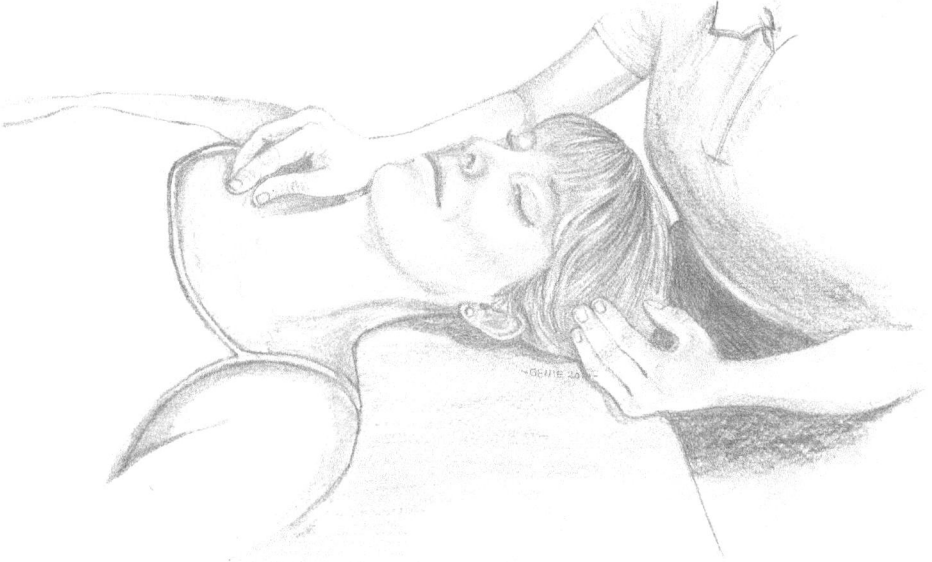

Illust. 7-21. Right clavicle to left side of head.

The hold position on the side of the head is located approximately two inches directly above the ear on a straight line from the ear to the top of the head (the parietal bone).

After sufficient time, reverse this hold, moving to the opposite clavicle and the opposite side of the head. [Illustration 7-22]

Illust. 7-22. Left clavicle to right side of head.

This set of holds expands the influence of the clavicle/jaw holds, further strengthening the structural grid of the cranium.

Jaw to Side of Head

Match hands on the sides of the head, keeping the holds very gentle. Then move one hand to the opposite jaw. [Illustration 7-23]

Illust. 7-23. Left side of head to right jaw.

...and [Illustration 7-24].

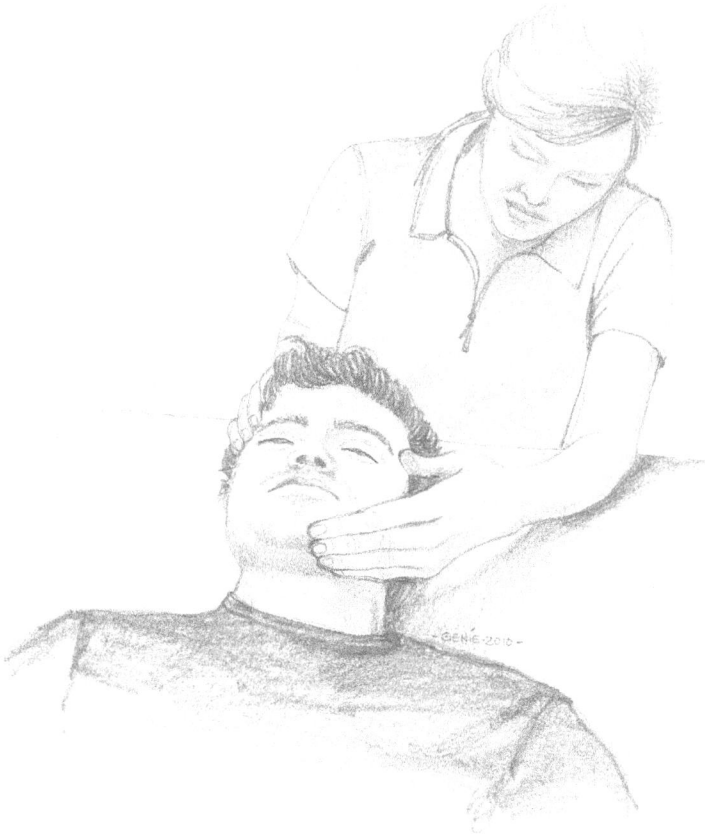

Illust. 7-24. Right side of head to left jaw.

This connection hold brings together your thoughts and communication, all the while further strengthening the cranial grid. These gentle facial holds also are working the craniosacral system, bringing it back into balance.

The therapist will notice a continual quieting of the systems. You may find that even if the client was talking through most of the Source Connection Therapy, he or she will become quiet during the holds involving the head. Match hands on the jaw and reverse this hold, repeating the holds on the other side.

Jaw to Brow

Match hands at the chin (jaw), then move one hand to the eyebrow. Gently touch with one or two fingers at the frontal bone next the bridge of the nose. This point on the brow is on the orbit of the frontal bone closest to the nose. [Illustration 7-25]

Illust. 7-25. Left jaw to right eyebrow.

...and [Illustration 7-26]. Transition by reversing holds to the opposite brow, then to the opposite jaw.

Illust. 7-26. Right jaw to left eyebrow.

Cheek to Brow

One hand remains in the same position on the brow and the other hand calmly and gently moves to the opposite cheek. After a moderate time, reverse holds to the opposite cheek, then the opposite brow. [Illustration 7-27]

Illust. 7-27. Right brow to left cheek.

...and [Illustration 7-28].

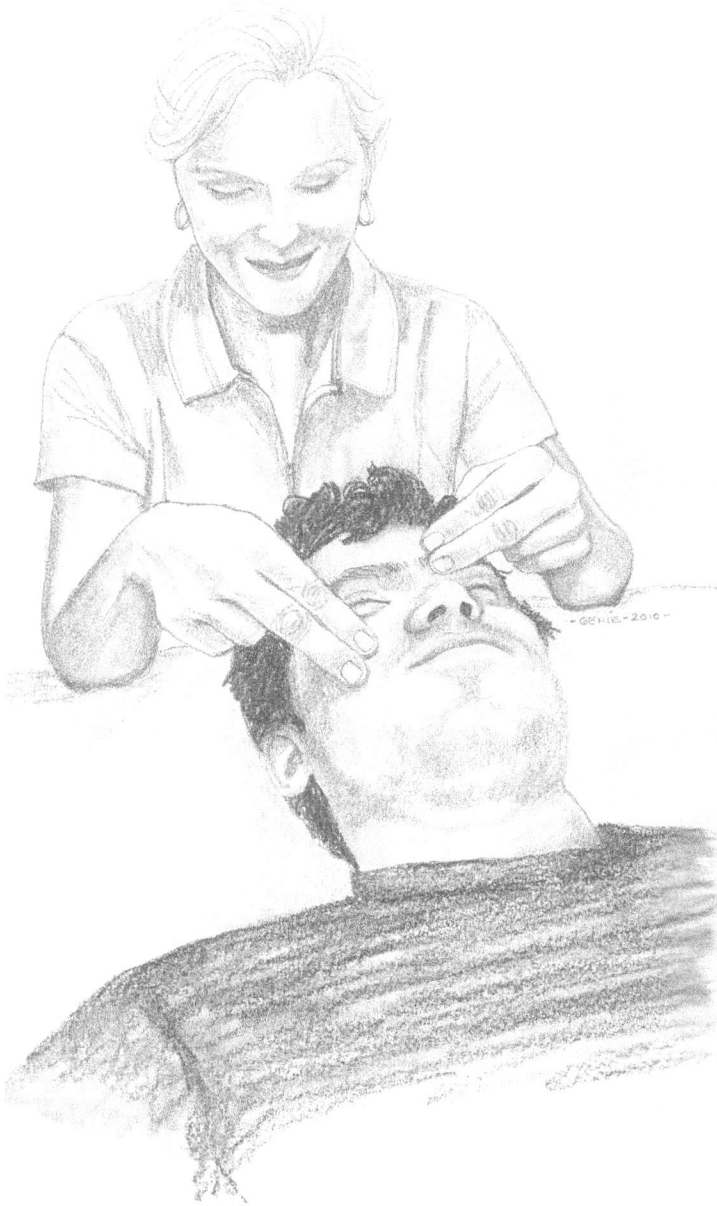

Illust. 7-28. Left brow to right cheek.

Brow to Earlobe

Match hands at the brow again, then move one hand to the opposite earlobe. Then match hands on the earlobes as a transition to the next hold. Move one hand from an earlobe to the opposite eyebrow. [Illustration 7-29]

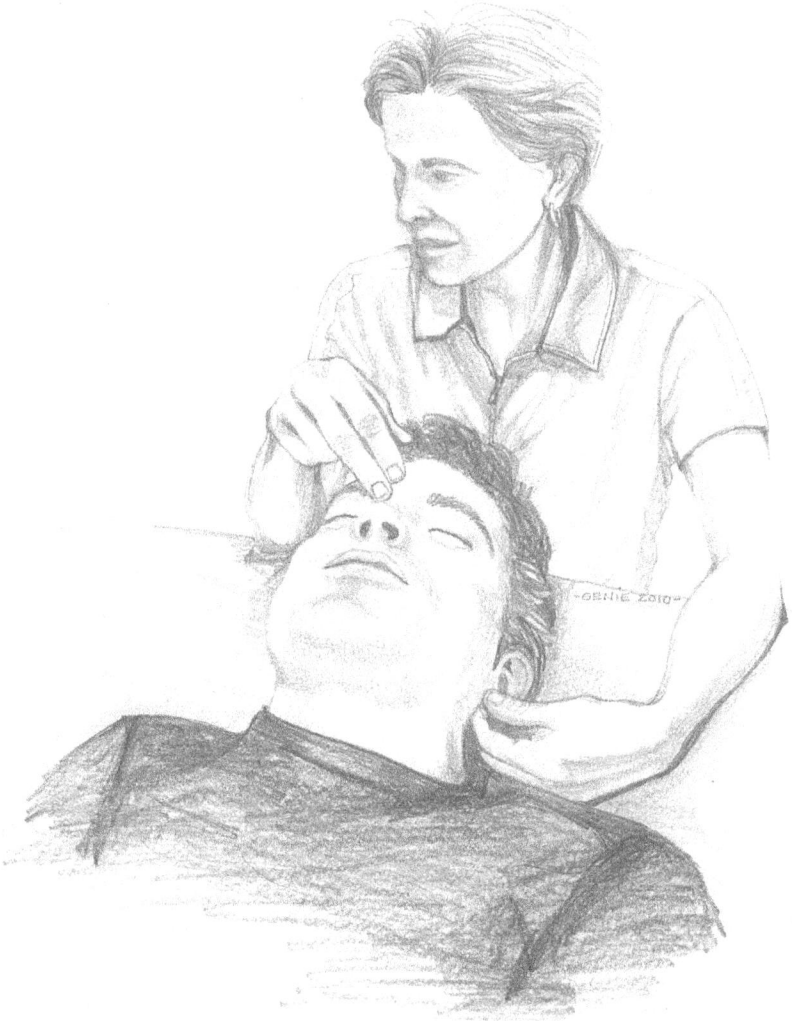

Illust. 7-29. Left earlobe to right brow.

...and Illustration 7-30]. Reverse holds, while maintaining gentle contact with the client. Remember to not lose contact.

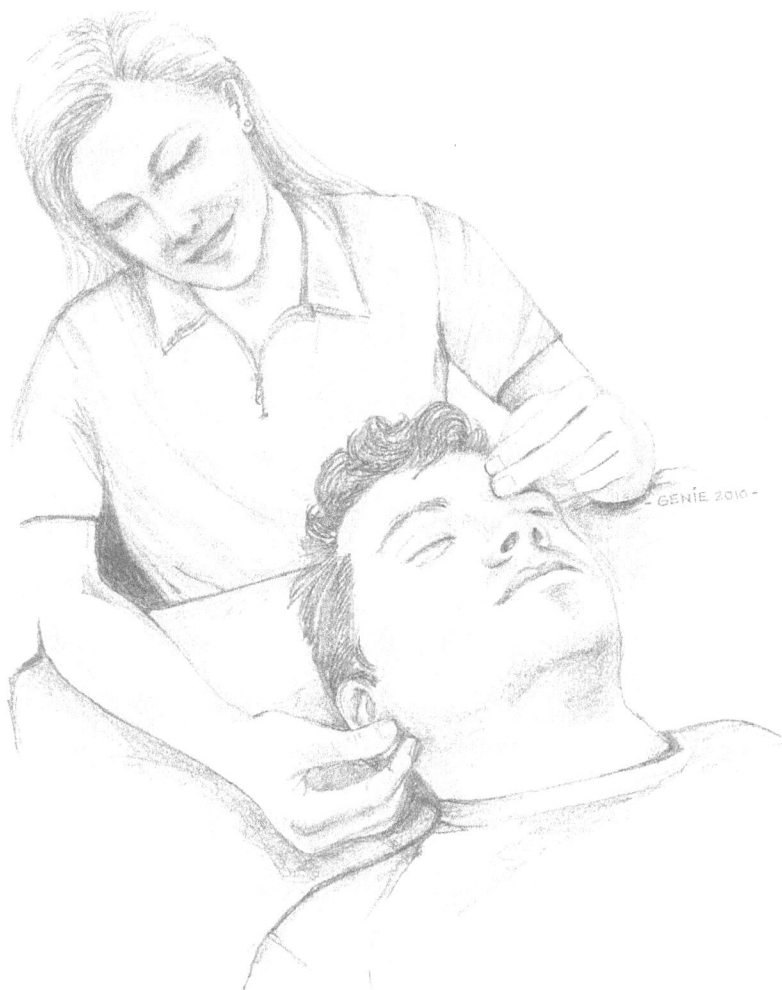

Illust. 7-30. Right earlobe to left brow.

Third Eye to Crown Chakra

The therapist should transition to this hold by matching hands on the brow, then moving one hand to the Third Eye—the center of the forehead. Next, move the other hand to the Crown Chakra, the center point on the top of the head. Use a very gentle touch with fingertips. [Illustration 7-31]

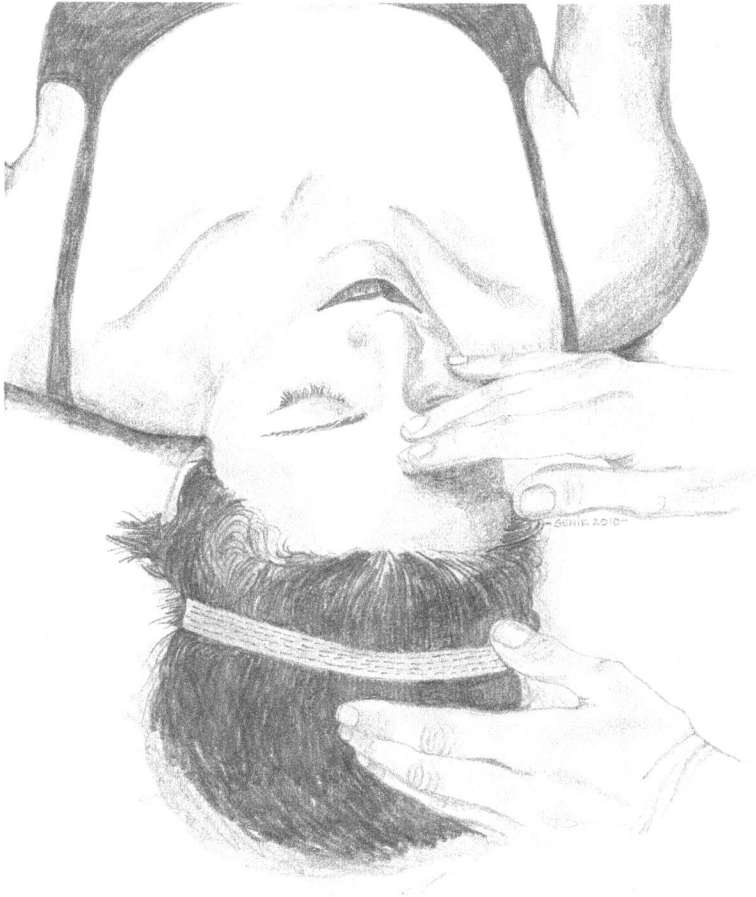

Illust. 7-31. Crown Chakra to Third Eye Chakra.

This hold is about intuition, which is your inner knowing, not just the physical world you visually see. This hold connects you to your Source by opening both the Third Eye Chakra and the Crown Chakra. As these two Chakras open and stay in balance, your communication with Source is clear so you can hear the guidance.

After performing the treatment protocol on another person, I always give them space by quietly moving back away from the client where I remain silent. Because the client is in a state of deep relaxation and may be almost in a dreaming mind-set, I remain focused on the person, ready to steady him.

Once the client is again alert and starting to move, you should always advise him or her to get up slowly and hold onto the side of the table or a chair. This advice is important because the client's restful circumstance will result in lowered blood pressure and a slowed heart rate. Standing suddenly can cause the client to become dizzy or even black out. There is no danger if the client rises to a sitting position and pauses for a minute or two before standing. Please be respectful, calm, and considerate of the client's physical and emotional feelings.

Conclusion

The impacts and benefits of the Source Connection Therapy are cumulative. The culmination of this connective therapy and doing this treatment on yourself or others daily has strong benefits because the body has cellular memory. The more frequently the body is reminded to reconnect or remain connected, the more effective the treatment. The implications of these cumulative effects on body, mind, and spirit are that you become a dynamic, self-contained being, who is closely aligned with your Source, open to receiving the information you need for a positive daily life. You are then able to move through your life, no matter the situation, in a calm and assertive manner that comforts yourself and others who are in your presence.

When the treatment is complete the client will feel physically relaxed as if she had taken a badly needed rest. She will feel clear and alert. With all of the points reconnected, the body is left in a positive, dynamic state.

Chapter 8
Responsibility of Being Balanced, The Sunny Side of the Street

Source Connection Therapy and the balance you can achieve should not be limited to yourself. To reach its greatest impact, Source Connection Therapy needs to be passed along to others. By being balanced yourself and helping others, you'll make the world a better place. My sincere belief is that you can do this, and as more and more people pass on the benefits of this therapy, the happier and healthier we will be.

Responsibility comes with Source Connection Therapy and being a balanced person. This is responsibility to self, others, and the planet. Accepting and living up to this responsibility becomes easier over time because you learn to listen more acutely, and are better able to hear and understand the messages you receive from Source and from the world around you. Importantly, you also learn to listen, hear, and understand the messages being sent to your mind by your body. You learn to be self-contained and less susceptible to negative inputs from outside of yourself.

Responsibility to Self

On The Sunny Side of the Street

Grab your coat and get your hat
Leave your worries on the doorstep
Life can be so sweet
On the sunny side of the street.

Can't you hear the pitter-patter?
And that happy tune is your step
Life can be so sweet
On the sunny side of the street.

I used to walk in the shade
With the blues on parade
But I'm not afraid
I'm crossing over and I'm walking in clovers.

If I never had a cent
I'd be rich as Rockefeller
with Gold dust at my feet
On the sunny side of the street.

Songwriters: Dorothy Fields, Jimmy Mchugh,
All rights by EMI Music Publishing Print Department

I love that song because it so clearly and positively describes a big part of my life. It also describes a major tenant of Source Connection Therapy—you can trade in those old unhealthy life patterns, for positive, healthy ones. If you find yourself walking in the shade feeling the blues, then maybe my experience can help you. I believe you can find happiness and serenity by taking control of your own life and asking for guidance from Source. You will be making your life the best possible. With your Source Connection, even if you're not in a bad situation, your life can improve. You can become healthier, happier, and more at ease with life.

You can be like happy-go-lucky Tigger, or you can be like terribly sad Eeyore, always walking under a dark cloud. I believe you can be more joyous and more certain of your higher self. I believe you can, by connecting to Source, find the guidance to direct you to a higher level. The choice is yours to make, and I would like to help.

The shady side of the street ultimately is depression. In severe situations, that shady side of the street can end tragically. In cases of abusive relationships, the shady side of the street may be physical and emotional injury, or worse. For any of you in those dire situations, please know that I understand what it's like and how terribly difficult it is to get free. Please also understand that you're worth saving; you can break free of negative influences and help yourself.

I *used to walk in the shade with the blues on parade*. But, if you asked people who knew me then, they wouldn't have said that about me. I was able to hide my blues. I was able to stave off depression because I was too busy proving to the world that I could make it and care for four kids. I hid my feelings by trying to be funny, making jokes about the things that were going so badly. When I was alone, though, my life was no joking matter. There was little happiness and not much genuine humor.

My husband, a habitual drinker, was frequently intoxicated. All the negative ramifications associated with that came true at one time or another. He had two kids and so did I—both sets of kids from prior marriages. Life held a lot of disappointment and let-downs. Because I couldn't depend on him, I took on the task of raising the four kids. Looking back on those ten years, I realize that being around the children, and trying so hard to do right by them, helped me in many ways.

During those years there were bright spots. I thoroughly enjoyed the children, and they gave me a physical release. The physical release, I realize now, also was an emotional vent, which allowed me to release the pent up anger and frustration. Without a physical activity to take me away from my daily life, I'm not sure I would have found the answers I so desperately needed.

I was a runner. I'd been a runner for many years before this relationship, and I'd learned to clear my mind of problems while running. During those years of dysfunctional marriage, I was happiest when running. Running was personal. Running gave me some self-esteem. I felt best about myself when I was running, and my peers recognized my ability as a good runner. Running allowed me to devote my effort to achieving something that was just for me, a personal activity with personal satisfaction. Finishing a marathon was a happy moment for me, regardless of where I placed.

You might say that running was my anti-depressant. And that may be more true than I'd suspected. Recent studies have shown clearly that activities such as exercise may be as effective as anti-depressant medications. In January 2010, The *Journal of American Medicine* (JAMA) reported that some anti-depressants are no more effective than placebo pills, exercise, or exposure to sunshine for patients who suffer from mild or moderate depression. Even an ice cream cone on a sunny day may be a more effective anti-depressant than Prozac, Paxil, and the rest. Take some time and research the studies. You'll find these over-prescribed drugs are often ineffective and expensive, and they frequently lead to increased suicidal thoughts and actual suicides. I believe you can find physical and emotional health in your life if you try to become balanced before looking to chemicals, which may only mask the underlying issues.

For others in bad situations who don't have a form of physical or emotional release at a personal level, life can be even worse. I was lucky. I also was lucky because I got out of the situation before too much damage had been done to my son and daughter and to me. For years friends told me to get out, to leave. Intellectually, of course, I knew they were right. Taking that step, however, is very difficult even when you're suffering. Leaving is difficult even when you recognize you're in danger. We hear about it all the time. You know mentally that you need to leave to try to salvage something of your own life, but emotionally it's not that easy. I thought I had to stay to help the kids. I thought I had a responsibility to see it through since I'd made the decision to marry this man. And whether consciously or subconsciously, I thought I could change things.

In retrospect, those ten years of dysfunctional marriage turned out to be the best thing for me. Why? Because I was forced to rely on something greater than myself. I was pushed to such extremes that I recognized I couldn't handle all of it alone.

Slowly and surely the answers to my questions were coming. As I described in the beginning of this book, I was skeptical, yet many of the answers I needed were there. Had I been in a tolerable situation, I may not have asked for help.

During those years in the shade, above all else, I wanted to know I was okay. I wanted some hint that I was accepted and respected by my peers. I had to learn to make each day the best day ever. Gradually, I did learn that and when I was given the gift of Source Connection Therapy, my life steadily improved. I connected with my personal Source, God, and from there I received the guidance I needed.

I fully recognize that not all of you consider God to be your source. That's okay. Source Connection Therapy isn't about religion; it's about belief and direction in your life. In fact, I believe it doesn't matter who or what you consider to be your Source, as long as you take the time and make the effort to reach a connection to someone or something outside of yourself. Whether you're a devotedly religious person or an atheist, the result can be the same. You can find guidance by focusing on a higher level.

Science or *Mother Nature* may hold the key to life's mysteries for you. If so, connect and learn from that. For many, there is a Universal Energy Field that emanates from and connects all living things, from the simplest microbes to the most complex mammals. If that is your belief, then embrace it and relish the fascination of these complexities, listening and finding your path from these Universal Energy Fields. Whether your beliefs are as a Christian, Muslim, Jew, Buddhist, Hindu, Native American or some other religion (or no religion at all), find your Source through your personal beliefs and allow that Source to answer your questions.

Regardless of your beliefs or your vision of Source, you must ask questions to get answers. Connect with your Source and ask for guidance, ask what path is right and then listen. It may take a long time, and it certainly will take an open mind and a balanced spirit.

After years of turmoil in my life that tried to pull me down and lock me in a dark, unhappy place, I recognized I had to become a balanced person. As I opened my mind to other possibilities and asked for help, I was shown how to cross over to the sunny side of the street.

I often tell people I knew *how to do,* but not *how to be.* I functioned as a human dynamo—a single parent for nine years and worked three to five jobs. Every day was stressful for me and the kids. Luckily, I ran nearly every day just to save what sanity I had. I was showing the world, damn it, that I could support my two kids alone. Driven to do more, to prove more, I nearly always felt that I wasn't doing a good job for the kids. Anyone in this circumstance needs help, but for a long time I was reluctant to ask. Finally, as I was hitting the wall, there was no choice but to seek help.

During all of this time, intellectually I convinced myself I was doing the right thing and the only thing I could. But, deep inside, I knew this wasn't a joyful person whom I saw in mirror. I felt genuine joy having my children with me, but something serious was lacking, preventing me from being joyous.

Through adversity, we either grow or we don't. It's the law of the land. This rover crossed over to the sunny side of the street where I remain today, every day. You can, too. And, let me tell you, it's worth the effort. Try it, then don't ever look back. Rather, make every day the best you can.

The sunny side can be joyous. For me, the sunny side of the street is not to carry the burdens of other people and other things on my back. During all of those dark years, a great deal of my burden was that I was carrying other people. I was compensating for my husband, lifting him up. Those burdens, rather than helping others, were just pushing me down. Now, I take the responsibilities of family, children, friendships, and work very seriously, but I'm no longer responsible for the problems and dysfunctional behavior of other people. I do what I can to help others, but the obligation for the outcome is theirs, not mine.

The sunny side of the street is waking up knowing life is good. It's knowing that whatever you have to do—whether delightful or drudgery— you can do it and do it well. At the end of even a very bad day, you can be a balanced person and accept the responsibility that comes with it.

With that responsibility comes the commitment to take care of yourself, keeping your physical, mental, and spiritual boundaries firmly protected to defend against the negatives that bombard you. You'll become aware of previously untapped energy within you and around you and the energy between you, other people, and the planet.

Every time we fly on a commercial airliner, the flight attendant reminds us that to be responsible for others, children, you should take care of yourself first: put the oxygen mask on yourself first before trying to assist others. Likewise, before you can help other people during your daily life, you need to care for yourself first. Balance yourself first, then reach out to others.

Just as you have a responsibility to yourself to brush your teeth daily, you also should balance yourself by applying the techniques of Source Connection Therapy, daily. Think of it as spiritual hygiene. Because of the cumulative effects of Source Connection Therapy, the benefits you achieve will be enhanced by regular practice. In some cases it may take several times through the protocol before you begin feeling and living the benefits. Think of the therapy as a long-term investment, sort of like a retirement account, where the more you put into it now, the longer you will enjoy its benefits.

As you feel inner peace—more relaxed and with a more positive attitude—your body will feel more together, organized, and vital. You'll enjoy heightened intuition and connection to Source as well as greater awareness of what your body needs to regain and maintain health. With regular use of Source Connection Therapy, the benefits become evident of a more open electro-magnetic energy field, a greater awareness of your balanced self, and an open connection with Source. You can more clearly see the direction your life should take. Your life will have more meaning; you'll feel more joy and gratitude. Isn't that what your life should be? How will you know your guidance is from Source? I gauge it by knowing that I'll never be told to do anything that will hurt me or anyone else.

When I speak or write about the concept of protection from negatives around us, I visualize boundaries. I see the boundaries as strong, positive energy fields that surround a balanced person like an invisible capsule, almost like a bubble.

Being surrounded by these strong, positive energy fields doesn't mean it blocks messages and input from outside. The boundary is not a barrier. In fact, the boundaries you establish are formed by your energetic body, with open Heart Chakra, open Third Eye Chakra, and open Crown Chakra. The barriers are strong, positive energy fields. The protection provided by the electro-magnetic field will deflect negative forces coming at you, and the open Chakras will allow input from Source and output to the earth. You will be grounded, comfortable in your energy patterns, and open to receive messages from your personal Source. Negative energies and negative people or situations will have little impact if you maintain the positive energy surrounding you.

You have a responsibility to yourself to take the time, make the effort, and pay attention to being healthy. Be good to yourself. Exercise as much as you reasonably can. Engage your mind in challenging activities like reading or writing or taking a class. Engage your right brain creativity in any way you can, even if it's simply listening to music or looking at fine art. And please, take your spiritual and emotional self seriously by connecting to your personal Source, striving for an elevated state of awareness.

You have a choice to walk on the sunny side of the street from now on. I know you can do it and I'm on your side. Go for it.

Responsibility to Others

You may think this seems contradictory, but the greatest responsibility you, as a balanced person, owe to other people is to stay out of their business. Your responsibility is to respect others' boundaries. If you think of yourself as enveloped by a positive energy field, yet being open to the world, then you can understand other people being the same. I'm not suggesting you disengage from people. I'm suggesting you, as a self-contained person, stand by someone else who is also self-contained, allowing a clean flow of energy communication between you. Respect others' comfort zones.

You may intuitively think the best thing to do for others is to give them advice, try to change them into what you envision as a better person. Asserting your will toward others to make them change will simply not work. You can't change another person by attempting to force your will and your ideas on them no matter how hard you try. You can, however, be a positive force for change in another's life by encouraging them and setting an example. Even having a positive attitude and open heart will influence those around you.

A friend related this story. I would like you to conduct an experiment and see if you don't find the same thing. Next time you go out, to work or shopping or to play, pay attention to the people you see. Ask yourself if they seem happy and comfortable, or if they seem frightened, closed off, or sad. Then remember the ones who appeared to be positive, out-going people and question if maybe they are the few balanced people in the larger number you encountered.

Here is my friend's story:

"I went shopping at a big box store this afternoon, even though it wasn't high on my list of fun things to do. As I drove into the lot, a woman with a shopping cart behind her was loading her car. I was blocked and she was unaware I was sitting there in my pickup waiting for her. A car pulled up behind me and only moments later honked his car horn. A very unhappy face looked at me from my rear view mirror. Still the woman with the cart didn't seem to notice us. Had she moved her cart about three feet, the driveway would have been clear.

"After I finally parked and was inside the store, I started to notice that the majority of people seemed unaware of what was going on around them. They blocked aisles, stood in front of displays even though others were trying to work around them. But, mostly, I noticed that very few people looked comfortable or happy. Not many smiles. I was catching some clips of negative conversations, and I was starting to feel really bummed. I just wanted to make my purchases and get out of there as quickly as possible.

"As I rounded a corner by the freezer section and looked down a very long aisle, I saw a woman who stood out from the masses. She was probably sixty feet away, yet she stood out from the others. She was smiling and standing straight. She had a little spring in her step and she radiated a positive mood. I stopped and watched, realizing that this one person, among so many, was spreading a wonderful, energetic feeling. She nodded at strangers and spoke kind words to nearly everyone she passed. I noticed that some of the frowning shoppers this woman interacted with smiled when she spoke to them and a few kept smiling after the woman had passed.

"When I said hello to her, intentionally trying to speak before she did, her face lit up and her smile widened. I felt a physical change come over me, I felt her electro-magnetic energy, her aura, touch me and influence me.

"She went on with her errands and I did with mine, but I was now smiling, and the edge of anxiety I had felt vanished. I felt good because this stranger's positive energy lifted me.

"We can, I am convinced, influence others by our actions. And, Genie, I was then smiling and nodding to people and saying hello to strangers."

Once you're balanced, you'll find it easy to be a friend, listening and taking seriously what others share with you and being empathetic. When people ask for help, being there for them, sharing your experiences and knowledge honestly will seem more natural without undue stress on your emotions when you are balanced yourself. When asked, you'll be willing to give your honest, informed opinion and provide all of the positive encouragement you can.

When working with another person using Source Connection Therapy or when helping a sick friend, don't be attached to the outcome. In many cases, the helping friend or the therapist (or the medical doctor) can't control the outcome. If you're attached to the outcome rather than the process to get there, a bad result likely will bring down your spirits, making the situation worse for the person you're trying to help. Helping a person who is terminally ill, for example, is a very important endeavor, but to be the most help, you'll need to focus on the treatments, the friendship, and encourage the client to live every day to the fullest.

In relationships with children and young people, a balanced person's obligations may require more active involvement. We all have a special responsibility to children. If your Source guides you to, providing greater direction with young people may be helpful. Your Source may show you that youngsters need guidance and teaching far beyond what may be appropriate for an adult. They may need someone to look up to who can mentor them in many different ways. If you are balanced and connected to Source, then your calm, assertive demeanor will enlist appropriate and consistent discipline with structure and love when you help a child. Keeping your core energies strong with Source guidance and approaching every situation with a young person from a viewpoint of success will pay off far more than negative, self-esteem-busting approaches.

For months, the fourteen-year-old daughter of a client had been in and out of doctors' treatment. She was diagnosed with a minor heart problem that was very real, yet the doctors didn't seem clear on what was causing her distress.

This girl was frequently sick and missed a lot of school. Her dad brought her to see me. I'd done Source Connection Therapy on him, so it was natural for him to think that balancing her might be beneficial. He was obviously worried.

I spent time talking with and listening to this beautiful girl. She was tense and reluctant to talk at first, but as we got acquainted she opened up a bit. She talked more about her feelings and what was going on at home.

In a short time of just listening carefully, I learned she was in the crosshairs of an energetic fight between her parents. They were going through a divorce, and their daughter was being torn apart by alliances on both sides. She was so fragmented that her literal body was crying out for someone to take charge and care for her.

I believe her heart problems were directly caused by her emotional self being ripped apart. In her sincere attempt to avoid hurting anyone's feelings, she was getting sick. She was holding in all the turmoil, and her body manifested this as illness.

I applied Source Connection Therapy, balancing her for an hour that first day, listening to her all the while. As I worked and she talked, I clearly saw her demeanor change, and I could feel her physical body relaxing and moving toward a more positive direction.

Appropriately, her heart condition is being monitored by her doctors, but she no longer has the heart-related symptoms that were so worrisome. Now, any illness she has is what one would expect with an average youngster in school. This great kid now asks her parents from time to time if she can come for a balancing treatment with Source Connection Therapy. I'm always happy to see her.

I'm thrilled that this teenager has worked through so much and seems so comfortable and balanced. She and her family now focus on positive aspects of her life.

Imagine a situation where you arrive home from a difficult day at work and you're tired. You just want to relax. Yet when you check phone messages, there's a call from the school telling you your child has a problem. What to do? Should you confront your child immediately? Probably not. Now is the time to balance yourself before talking with your child.

Take at least five minutes and settle yourself before you approach your child. Be aware that your child also will not be balanced, having been in a classroom all day, facing peer pressure and whatever caused the problem. The best way to help balance your child is to start by balancing yourself. The results, I suspect, will be much more successful.

With all relationships, the best result will occur when you help him or her become a strong, balanced person.

My hope is that through practicing Source Connection Therapy you will become self-contained, filled with love and joy so you can help others. What you give back is that love and joy and those will affect other people. With daily practice of Source Connection Therapy you'll establish a strong core energy and start living in a self-contained space, becoming independent, strong, and joyous. Being balanced will emit positive, loving feelings to others without invading their space.

I was traveling from my home in northern Idaho to California where I had a full schedule of treatments booked. At the Spokane Airport, I checked in and wanted to check my massage table, a folding table made specifically for traveling.

That morning must have been going badly for the counter agent because he showed no sign of being friendly or helpful. He measured my table and told me it could not be checked because it was too large.

"I've traveled with this table for years," I told him. "No one has ever questioned its size until now. Is there something we can do?"

His reply was curt, insulting, and over-flowing with anger and negativity. At first, I wondered if it was me, but then I saw that he was rude to others, as well. After several minutes of frustration for both of us and a lot of anger-venting by the airline employee, my table was checked. I got a boarding pass, and I moved on toward the departure lounge

I could feel the impact of his negativity as I walked up a ramp and dreaded my next encounter with TSA screening. I felt edgy. The man's strong negative energy had gotten to me. Even as I fought it, trying to regain my normal happy state, I could feel the poison of his negative energy. I grumbled to myself and felt as if I had a black cloud hanging over my head. I felt like Eeyore. Obviously, I wasn't fully in balance. My own protective energies were weak at the time.

I cleared security and moved toward the plane, feeling sorry for myself. I looked ahead and made eye contact with the flight attendant and smiled as best I could. She smiled back. Her genuine smile was like a searchlight guiding me into friendly territory. She obviously was a balanced person.

At my seat, I took a quick inventory and realized I was no longer smiling, I was glum and my feelings were hurt by how I'd been treated. I must have looked upset because the flight attendant who had caught my eye smiled again. Her smile was warm and confident and immediately I could sense the positive energy surrounding her. Her smile was followed by an offer to bring me water. I said, "Sure. Water would be nice."

The flight attendant went far beyond her required job duties and engaged me in pleasant conversation, handed me a small plastic cup of water and smiled again. I could feel my hurt subsiding. A smile was edging its way onto my face. Two more times, the attendant came back to me with a positive attitude and a kind, happy smile. She gave me a full can of cold water, turning my negative experience into something positive.

"You just changed everything. You changed all of the negative energy that was here into something good," I told her.

More than simply changing a bad situation into something good, she reminded me that the hurt and dark energy I felt was partially my fault. My responsibility to myself was to not carry the negatives of others with me.

This experience clearly shows both our responsibility to ourselves and the responsibility we have to others.

I had, in fact, allowed the counter agent's negativity to get inside me. I had let my personal responsibility wane for a bit. I allowed myself to get out of balance and be susceptible to the negative energy that affected me. I had, for a short time, allowed myself to become less than self-contained, something that is important for me to avoid.

The angry agent had failed in his responsibility to me by treating me with disrespect and by erupting with negative energy. He had directed his unhappiness and anger squarely at me. Beyond that, he had failed his responsibility to himself by allowing his mood to sour and affect his work.

The flight attendant, however, was perfectly complying with her responsibility to herself, being positive and strong and aware. She met her responsibility to others by being alert and aware of my feelings and taking action to make things better for me. She changed my attitude and awakened me to the need to get back into balance. She did these things not by interfering or telling me what to do; rather, she treated me with kindness and respect. She smiled, releasing a flood of good energy my way, and she followed through with some positive action and kind words.

I took on my responsibility and balanced myself during the flight south, using the techniques I shared in Chapter 6.

I don't suggest you place yourself at risk of harm, but if you see another person in trouble, ask your Source if you can help. If it's the right thing, you'll know internally. Let your Source guide you. Lend a hand whenever you are guided to do so. Your responsibility to self and to others overlaps or coincides. Treat yourself with respect. Treat others with respect.

Responsibility to Community and Earth

Responsibility to community and Earth is to be balanced, to act honestly and responsibly. You'll be guided to think for yourself, arriving at conclusions that affect your community and the planet based on facts and honesty. I encourage you to do your own research, think for yourself while asking Source for guidance. Then act according to your own belief structure. I hope you become a free thinker and stand up for those beliefs, especially during this time of twenty-four-hour news channels and talk radio. We should expect truth, and we should only share truth.

As a balanced person, it will be easy to take on the responsibility of making your community and the planet better, even in the simplest ways. Here's an example: I'm an avid hiker and rock climber. While hiking in Washington State, I watched a young woman throw a candy wrapper on the ground. She didn't drop it by mistake, or fail to notice when it slipped out of her hand. She intentionally wadded it up and tossed it.

"Do you always throw your trash on the ground?" I asked her.

"It's only one piece of paper and not even that big," she replied.

"Let's suppose a hundred people come by here today, each with a piece of garbage. And imagine that the next person sees your litter there." I pointed to the candy wrapper on the grass. "So, that person says to herself, someone threw trash there, so will I. And, she throws her piece of trash beside yours. Then, the next and the next and the next until a hundred pieces of trash are piled there. What do we have now? A pile of garbage. Yet, each part of the pile, as you said, is only one piece and not very big, at that."

The young woman looked at me, then at the wrapper. She didn't say anything.

"I'm not telling you what to do," I said calmly. "But, I am asking you to decide for yourself what your personal standards in this situation are. Is this really the kind of place you want? Do you want to live and hike and play among piles of garbage?" I smiled and tried to hurl my most positive energy her way.

She smiled back at me, as if a reflection of my own grin. She picked up the candy wrapper, jammed it in her jeans pocket and nodded to me as she moved on the trail.

"Thanks," I said. "Pass it on."

The littering example is such a small thing, but I think it shows we can take a stand in a positive way and influence others to take care of our communities and our planet.

Some people's lives are complete when they stay home and even avoid interaction with the planet. Yet sometimes we see examples of individuals doing interesting, even remarkable things for the environment or for other species. The difference, I believe, is that people are guided in different directions by their personal Source. I'm not suggesting everyone who becomes balanced must get out and do remarkable things for the planet. I do believe that at one time or another each of us will be guided to help. I'm reminded of the power of the individual toward our planet by the following example.

For a few years a mated pair of Bald Eagles have resided at a state park where I often hike. The male eagle injured his wing and was unable to fly. A volunteer took it upon himself to save the eagle. Not only did the man provide first aid and gentle care, but he investigated how the injury occurred in the first place and determined the bird had flown low and hit a wire fence at the park boundary.

The injury was a sprained wing, and the Bald Eagle recovered at a rehab center about thirty miles away. The good Samaritan picked up the recovered eagle from the center and kept it at his home near the park for about a week. During that week, the female eagle frequently circled the man's house and was circling when the male bird was released inside the park.

At his own expense and with an investment of many hours, this one man made a difference to our community by saving this Bald Eagle. But it was only one bird. What difference could just one bird make? The same as the candy wrapper. If a hundred good Samaritans take action and rescue an injured bird, or an abandoned animal, fix up a playground, or help clean up a vacant lot, then the results are truly noticeable. A balanced, self-contained person will take these types of actions, making the community and the planet better. And if each person affected by these acts of kindness and care passes it on, the results can be extremely good for us all. When you send your positive energy back to the Earth, only good can come of it.

At a global level, it obviously is difficult for an individual to make a difference. But like the Bald Eagle and the candy wrapper, if thousands of balanced people worked together, perhaps systemic changes can be made.

Personal responsibility is asking the right questions and learning what to rely on and what things to avoid. As with the responsibility to others, on the larger scale of community and planet, each balanced person needs to drive his or her own car. Take care of yourself and your own, but be ready to help others when guided to do so.

If you're a person who is self-contained and confident, you will educate yourself rather than believing other people's words. You'll examine the facts and evaluate how events are impacting your life and your community in reality. Because you, as a balanced person, come from a place of inner guidance, accepting messages from your personal Source, you will work for solutions that will enrich your life and your community.

Because you're balanced and working with both right and left brain hemispheres, seeing things through the prism of intuition and truth, you won't spread falsehoods or encourage fear. But you will be willing and able to be a calm, assertive person who can make a genuine beneficial difference. Source Connection Therapy can help individuals attain balance and to view themselves, others, and their communities in an honest, realistic way. Then, like the candy wrapper example, the impacts can spread as people share the benefits of balancing.

History clearly has taught us that passivity allows aggression to expand if we ignore the thugs and the bullies. We know without a doubt that aggression breeds aggression on an interpersonal level or international level. With Source guidance, responsibility—whether between two people, in a family, or internationally—will come with calm assertiveness, led by people who have achieved a level of balance.

As a balanced person, you find it easy to question everything, analyze information based on facts and then draw your own line between what is right for you and what is not. Whether you're seeking answers to personal life questions or wondering which way our nation should move, those answers will come only if you ask your Source and then listen with an open mind. Ask questions of your Source as you reach greater balance and self-awareness through Source Connection Therapy.

Answers will come from your Source. My personal Source, God, sees everyone equally and will provide honest answers to my sincere questions. Your Source will, too, no matter who you may be. As you look at the big picture and how you fit in with the larger world, you should recognize that because of our minds and our technologies, humans no longer interact with the world as we once did. We no longer naturally fit within the animal kingdom. In fact, humans are no longer part of evolution. In the animal world, the pack tries to balance each of its members. A wolf, for example, who is out of balance with the pack most likely will die, or be abandoned if it does not fall in line. In the animal kingdom, the strong survive and the weak do not. With humans, though, the slowest and the weakest are nurtured.

Because balancing is no longer a natural process for humans, we find that huge numbers of us are out of balance and out of control. We also find that because balance no longer comes naturally to our species, each of us needs to take the time and make the effort to become self-contained and balanced.

We may not solve these larger problems within our lifetimes, but as individuals we can fix ourselves and become positive, energetic, and balanced people. Perhaps, our greatest responsibility to the planet is to be balanced and do the best we can with the abilities we were given.

Although it may take some time because of the cumulative effects of Source Connection Therapy, be confident that you can attain tangible results. As your Heart, Third-Eye, and Crown Chakras are opened and your electro-magnetic energy fields strengthen, you will connect to Source and be grounded to Earth. As your energy fields strengthen, your left and right brain hemispheres will reunite and coordinate efficiently. When you achieve this level of balance and comfort, you'll be able to listen for the answers you seek. You will find guidance to your higher self. From there, my hope is you will spread the message of Source Connection Therapy.

Pass it on.

Go Forth

If you remain fragmented in your life you'll be tugged and pulled around by the debris that accumulates during life. We all have it. Physical, mental, and emotional damage easily can result if you don't learn how to discard the old, negative garbage from your life and make room for some new, positive stuff. Just like cleaning the garage, you need to throw out the old stuff to make room for the good stuff. Here's an example that may bring home the idea that this unwanted junk we tug along may be a serious health problem.

While I was writing this book, I traveled to California to help a friend who was having a Transient Ischemic Attack (TIA, commonly called a warning or mini stroke, which is caused from blood flow to the brain being cut off. She had all of the classic symptoms of a minor stroke, yet these symptoms—dizziness, tingling in her left arm, headaches—varied and cycled from very severe requiring hospitalization to nearly non-existent. Her doctor sent her home with a blood pressure cuff and required her to monitor her blood pressure.

As we sat in her living room and talked, my friend's blood pressure appeared normal, and she said she felt almost no symptoms related to her TIA. She seemed fine to me, and it felt good to sit with an old friend and chat about good times. As the topics moved toward more personal things in her life, she talked about family problems and long-ago issues she'd never discarded. Her blood pressure rose.

She was digging up debris of the kind we all carry around. She is a driven person with *"a take no prisoners"* approach to life. Her personality is strong, and she is constantly working from one project to another without taking a break for her own relaxation. Yet, my friend can always find time for others and listen to their problems, even though it often means adding to her own emotional baggage.

As we drove to the ocean, she again talked of by-gone problems. Stress symptoms reappeared, and I had to drive. Later, when we sat on the beach watching the Pacific surf, she calmed a bit, but the topic turned back to uncomfortable issues, and she appeared concerned about her health and discouraged to be in this situation. Her discomfort was almost like an anxiety attack.

My friend told me that the tests done at the hospitals, including an MRI, showed no real cause for TIA—such as blocked artery or bleeding in the brain. When she told me the doctors gave her an anti-anxiety medication at the hospital, this was a clue the whole episode may be directly related to an emotional barrier that manifested as a physical problem. I believe her physical problem was the result of an imbalance between her physical, mental, and emotional selves.

My good friend, like so many of us, carries way too much junk from the past. She did the correct thing by consulting with medical doctors. In conjunction with her medical care, I believe if she were to regularly balance herself she could more easily keep her blood pressure in a safe range.

In my practice, I commonly see clients with situations similar to my friend's. They have real physical symptoms, yet their doctors are unable to pinpoint a cause. In cases like this, the medications doctors prescribe simply mask the symptoms or make the patient feel as if he or she is cured. With many of these clients, they have become free of prior complaints after a few of my treatments. The reason: the physical symptoms, like my friend's, were not originally caused by a disease or injury. They were the result of an underlying imbalance among the physical, mental, and emotional selves to the point they were manifested as physical. Louise Hay refers to these physical manifestations caused by emotional imbalances in her book, *Heal Your Body*.

As I work with clients, I sometimes wonder what other applications there may be for Source Connection Therapy and its associated techniques. The following are some of my thoughts on where I would like to go from here.

Earlier in this book, I wrote about successes I've seen with various symptoms of Fibromyalgia. Obviously, much more work and study need to be done, but I continue to see improvement in clients who for years have suffered some or all of those symptoms, including pain and chronic fatigue.

As experience with Source Connection Therapy expands, I see a future where, in concert with other modalities and physicians, this therapy may make a difference in many situations. Here are a few that I would like to investigate further:

- **Addictions**. Drug and alcohol problems plague families and entire communities. My personal experience living with someone with these excesses makes me realize that balancing on a daily basis can help moderate the problem. Mostly, I have found in my practice that people undergoing rehab often are frightened and stressed. Source Connection Therapy has helped several people through this tough time.

- **Post Traumatic Stress Disorder**. The quieting effect, the turning inward and the building of positive electro-magnetic energy fields through Source Connection Therapy have initially shown some benefits. Somato Emotional Release from balancing with Source Connection Therapy should help fix tissue memory problems, which linger from prior injury or stress.

- **ADHD**. Studies show that various attention problems can be overcome through educational kinesiology. Because of the similarity of movement crossing the mid-line of the body, I believe a Source Connection Therapy protocol, especially self-help therapy, can benefit young people with ADHD symptoms, probably much better than medication.

- **Counseling**. I've seen instances where Source Connection Therapy balancing in conjunction with counseling can help a therapist achieve greater results than counseling alone.

- **Integrated Medicine**. Whether being treated for injury or disease, patients benefit from integration of typical western medicine and alternatives such as acupuncture, therapeutic massage, and Source Connection Therapy. In serious cases, such as cancer and stroke, the spirit-lifting aspects of Source Connection Therapy can help a patient live a higher quality life.

- **Enhanced Healing**. When the body, mind, and spirit are brought into homeostasis, the body's natural ability to heal will be enhanced. Whether for someone going through detox, or recovering from an accident or disease, relying on Source Connection Therapy can make the experience easier and less fearsome.

- **Dementia/Alzheimer's**. Studies indicate the physical exercises that force a dementia sufferer to move and connect across the body—left hand to right knee, for example—awaken cerebral connections. Similar movements and connections occur during Source Connection Therapy.

- **Prisons and Half-Way Houses**. Where anti-social behavior is a core problem, a person or population may benefit from Source Connection Therapy in several ways, including learning self-relaxation techniques, learning to be self-contained, and becoming a more balanced, whole person. Young offenders may benefit the greatest from balancing and learning to take care of themselves and to respect the boundaries of others.

July 2009, I taught a class in Seattle, Washington. This was a sixteen-hour introductory class to Source Connection Therapy, normally limited to professional therapists. For the past two years, I opened the class to anyone wishing to balance himself or herself as well as to therapists. I conduct the class to allow people to learn self-treatment and to share it with others. Therapists learn to use the protocol in their private practices.

A few days after I returned home to Idaho, I received a phone call from a psychologist in Seattle. One of her clients was among my students for that weekend. The counselor was seeking information on what I had done during the course. Basically, she was asking, "What did you do with my client?"

The counselor inquired because she'd seen such a marked improvement in her client from the last time they had met. She wanted to know more details about my Source Connection Therapy. Her client was far more positive, clearly focused, and confident than before the Source Connection Therapy class. These were changes the patient and psychologist had been working on for a long time.

The counselor was so amazed at the positive results of my class that she traveled to Idaho to learn the Source Connection Therapy technique to use with her own clients. She felt the therapy was vital in helping promote the personal growth and the balance of the clients' body, mind, and spirit. In her practice, in addition to her normal treatment regimen, this psychologist now includes Source Connection Therapy. She also teaches her clients how to do the therapy on themselves. She continues to see remarkable results and positive outcomes.

I routinely work with physical therapy patients who are referred to me by clinics. In nearly every case, the patient's recovery progresses more rapidly after they are engaged in Source Connection Therapy. The medical patient also benefits from Source Connection Therapy because a therapist like me takes time to listen, to learn who the patient really is. What I learn often leads to the discovery of underlying problems, which are either a cause or something inhibiting recovery. In some cases, I learn the patient is simply frightened.

I'm certain my therapy helps these and other clients feel better inside. Because they feel better about themselves, many find it easier to get through the recovery experience. They are more able to handle working through issues once they learn more about themselves.

Some medical doctors and physical therapy clinics are so over-burdened they don't have the luxury of time and personal contact to get to know their patients. Often because of these time restraints, patient's underlying fears and problems aren't recognized, resulting in roadblocks to true recovery.

Source Connection Therapy facilitates the healing process. A trained therapist will listen and know his or her client's underlying needs. Together, that therapist, the client, and Source Connection Therapy can make a huge, life-long difference one client at a time. An individual seeking better health and a more balanced life can do the same.

Pass it on.

Illust. 7-32. Genie working with baby alpaca.

About The Author

Genie Monte-Pelizzari is a licensed massage practitioner and Reiki Master with over twenty years of practical experience. She is a certified specialist in Myofascial Release, Craniosacral Therapy, Somato Emotional Release and Movement Therapy. Genie is an experienced instructor and curriculum developer for professional licensing programs in massage therapy.

Source Connection Therapy is the creation of Ms. Monte-Pelizzari, perfected over time and proven effective through working with hundreds of clients whom she helped find balance in their lives. She developed Source Connection Therapy with the specific goal of helping her clients achieve optimal health.

Genie is well known as the developer and teacher of this beneficial modality and uses Source Connection Therapy in her daily practice. She also travels to health shows and seminars. Genie is motivated by a strong desire to help others attain wellness, balance, and harmony in their lives by learning how to identify the Source in their own lives and then how to connect with that Source for effective healing and personal growth.

She discovered balance in her life through a close connection with her Source, God. From this personal revelation, she followed the guidance from her Source and developed a therapy through which others can achieve the same sense of wellbeing.

Genie is an avid rock climber and outdoor enthusiast. She balances her busy professional life with active adventures into the mountains near her northern Idaho home and the Pacific Northwest.

Source Connection Therapy is Genie's gift to others, a carefully thought out, meticulously-presented book encouraging others to find their personal Source and then attain full healing potential by using the connection techniques presented in this book.

www.sourceconnectiontherapy.com

Cited Works

Brennan, Barbara Ann. Hands of Light. New York: Bantam Books, 1988.

Eden, Donna, with Feinstein, David. Energy Medicine. New York: Penguin Group, 2008.

Gerber, Richard, MD. Vibrational Medicine. Santa Fe, NM: Bear & Company, 1988.

Hay, Louise L. Heal Your Body. Carlsbad, CA: Hay House, Inc., 1984.

McCraty, Rollin; Bradley, Raymond Trevor; Tomasino, Dana. "The Resonant Heart." SHIFT: At the Frontier of Consciousness, (December - February 2005): 15-19.

Millan, Cesar, and Peltier, Melissa Jo. Be the Pack Leader, New York: Harmony Books, 2007.

Taylor, Jill Bolte. My Stroke of Insight, New York: Penguin Group (USA), Inc., 2008.

Suggested Reading

Brennan, Barbara Ann. Light Emerging. New York: Bantam Books, 1993.

Calais-Germain, Blandine. Anatomy of Movement. Seattle, WA: Eastland Press, 1993.

Gawain, Shakti. Creative Visualization. San Rafael, CA: New World Library, 1978.

Gertz, S. David. Liebman's Neuroanatomy Made Easy and Understandable. Fifth Edition, New York: Aspen Publishers, 1996.

Gordon, Richard. Your Healing Hands. Oakland, CA: Wingbow Press, 1978.

Kluger, Jeffrey, ed. Your Brain: A User's Guide. New York: Time Books, 2009.

Lipton, Bruce H. 5th edition, The Biology of Belief. United States: Hay House, Inc., 2009.

Millan, Cesar, and Peltier, Meliisa Jo. Cesar's Way. New York: Three Rivers Press, 2006.

Milne, Hugh. The Heart of Listening 1. Berkley, CA: North Atlantic Books, 1995.

Milne, Hugh. The Heart of Listening 2. Berkley, CA: North Atlantic Books, 1995.

Stein, Diane. Essential Reiki. 8th printing, Freedom, CA: The Crossing Press, Inc, 1997.

To Contact the Author

For information on setting up lectures, classes in Source Connection Therapy, and SCT Teaching Certification classes, contact...

Genie Monte-Pelizzari LMP
PO Box 1243
Sandpoint, Idaho 83864
geniemp@yahoo.com
www.sourceconnectiontherapy.com

Notes:

www.ingramcontent.com/pod-product-compliance
Lightning Source LLC
Chambersburg PA
CBHW052106090426
42741CB00009B/1692